5·4·77

House Journal Editing

House Journal
Editing

BY

Ralph C. Darrow

SCHOOL OF JOURNALISM
KENT STATE UNIVERSITY
KENT, OHIO

ORDER FROM

The Interstate
Printers & Publishers, Inc.

DANVILLE, ILLINOIS 61832

Library of Congress catalog card number: 73-93505

Reorder No. 1628

PREFACE

In-house journalism, one phase of public relations, is a large and growing field. As organizations become large and complex, they are forced to use company-produced publications to communicate with various publics--internal and external. Internal publics include employees, salesmen, etc., or groups which are directly dependent upon the organization. External publics include customers, the general public, etc., or groups which owe no direct allegiance to the company.

Until comparatively recent times, there was no formal training for industrial journalism. The company which sought an in-house editor recruited one from a nearby newspaper. Now, more and more would-be editors are being trained for the job through college training courses.

The problem for many colleges in teaching such courses is the shortage of texts. It is hoped that this text fills that need.

One problem in preparing such a book is finding a title or name for the house journal.

The term "house organ," which has been widely used to describe such a publication, makes some practitioners cringe. The name "industrial publication" really would not apply to a mercantile or other non-industrial organization. "House magazine" is a misnomer if the company prints a newspaper. "Company publication" would not apply to a journal produced by a college but, as Shakespeare said, "What's in a name?" The author feels the term "house organ" is a specific and well-understood one to describe a publication produced by any organization for its own use.

"House" takes its name from the former great mercantile houses or companies of Europe, such as the House of Rothschild. "Organ" is an instrument of.

Because many in-house editors have a strong dislike for the term "house organ," the author has used the term "house journal" to describe this type of publication.

The author gratefully acknowledges the invaluable assistance of Mort Leggett, Supervisor of Employee Publications, The Goodyear Tire & Rubber Company, who painstakingly read through the manuscript and offered several good suggestions. Mort also located several good stories from The Wingfoot Clan, Goodyear Go, and Goodyear Perspective to illustrate types of stories found in house journals. In addition, he furnished several illustrations for use in the book, and permission to use the material.

Thanks go to Dr. Karl F. Treckel of the Kent State University Economics Department for taking time to read the manuscript and offering valuable comments upon the contents.

Thanks are also expressed to Robert Hoover, Public Relations Director of the Maytag Company, Newton, Iowa, for permission to use the <u>Maytag</u> <u>Bulletin</u> as an example. In addition, the author is grateful for permission to use materials from: Barberton Citizen's Hospital, Roadway Express, Inc., The Firestone Tire & Rubber Company, <u>Editor</u> <u>&</u> <u>Publisher</u>, The General Tire & Rubber Company, and The B. F. Goodrich Company.

Thanks go to the International Association of Business Communicators for permission to search its files.

The author acknowledges the invaluable assistance of his wife, Fae, who supplied much gentle arm twisting over a period of two years, aided greatly in the editing, and typed the manuscript at least twice.

CONTENTS

Chapter

1

HISTORICAL—THE NEED DEVELOPS

House journal editing, although allegedly engaged in as far back as the Han Dynasty in China 2,000 years ago, actually is a recent phenomenon, tied in with the growth of the world from an agrarian to a technological society.

There are no exact figures on how many house journals are published in the world. The International Association of Business Communicators has estimated there are approximately 12,000 industrial publications, worldwide, reaching a total audience of 500,000 per issue.

Gebbie House Magazine Directory in 1968 estimated the number of house journals or company publications at 50,000, reaching a total audience of approximately 180 million in the United States.

One of the first house journals in the United States was the Lowell Offering of the Lowell Cotton Mills, Lowell, Massachusetts. It was first produced in 1840 as an outlet for the literary expression of the company's female workers. Many of the company's employees were ex-school teachers who went to work in the mills because of the comparatively high wages. Some of the contributors subsequently won literary standing among American writers. (Willis Wisler, _Study of Content and Arrangement of Employee Magazines_, Columbus, Ohio, The Ohio State University Press, 1930, p. 1.)

A similar magazine, _The Mechanic_, was published from 1847 until 1914 by the H. B. Smith Machine Company of Smithville, New Jersey.

Other early company publications were _The Travelers Record_, started March 1, 1865, by James G. Batterson, founder of the Travelers Insurance Company, and _The Locomotive_, founded in 1867 by the Hartford Steam Boiler Inspection and Insurance Company. Both were highly successful. The _Record_ reached a circulation of 50,000 copies to rival in readership the leading popular magazines of the day.

These pioneer publications in industrial journalism were basically external in nature. The first true employee publication, according to today's standards, probably was _The Triphammer_, started in 1885 by the Massey-Ferguson Company. (Willis Wisler, _Study of Content and Arrangement of Employee Magazines_, Columbus, Ohio, The Ohio State University Press, 1930.)

A study made by the National Industrial Conference Board in 1925 listed the _Factory News_ of the National Cash Register Company as the earliest employee magazine. (_Employee Magazines in the United States_, National Industrial Conference Board, Inc., New York, 1925.)

Now known as the _NCR Factory News_, it is still going strong as one of this country's leading employee publications. It was established in 1890 as a 12-page monthly, but now often has as many as 7 to 10 times its original number of pages.

The house journal or company publication seems to be here to stay, although there have been drastic retrenchments during certain economically depressed years.

Organizations which have valid reasons for having company publications usually retain those publications fairly intact regardless of the financial climate. Such organizations recognize the need to communicate with their various publics.

On the other hand, the company publication of an organization which has not defined the need will often go under at the first sign of financial trouble.

The difference is that the company which recognized the need to communicate went into the program fairly well informed. However, many smaller companies may start a company publication without establishing a need. Because other companies are publishing one, management may decide to get on the bandwagon and publish. Since such an organization had no sound reason for having a publication, the company may cut off the journal as the first step of retrenchment.

Aside from any considerations of faddism or jumping on the bandwagon by managements, the steady growth of the company publication has occurred because of necessity. There is a vital need to communicate, and that need is created because organizations in America have tended to evolve from the simple to the complex.

In the early days of the republic, this country was agrarian. Industry was simple, usually a shop run in the home, or a backyard shop run by a man and his helper.

With such a simple business structure, communications could be carried out face to face. The boss saw his hired help each working day. The two knew each other well. Problems of wages, working hours, benefits, were discussed man to man, and mutual agreements were reached in a matter of minutes.

In this situation, the hired help probably was as well informed as the boss about problems which beset the business. If customers didn't pay their bills, the helper probably knew it as soon as the boss. In all aspects of the business, communications were swift and uncomplicated.

Contrast that with life today. Now the typical organization is a multi-national conglomerate producing and selling a diversity of goods and services. Some organizations are literally so huge that it defies the comprehension of many persons to understand the scope of the operations. Virtually all aspects of American life are organized on a large scale. The same situation exists or is building in much of the world. There are mergers of companies, unions, churches, schools, and other educational units.

When an organization has more than 100 production units operating in dozens of nations, employing 100,000 persons or more, and producing and selling several thousand products, plus several thousand sales outlets and salesmen in even more countries, communicating becomes a very complicated process.

Just the problem of communicating to the employees of one production factory is a complication.

Typically, in manufacturing industry, operations must be carried out around the clock. This means various employees are on the job for six- to eight-hour shifts throughout the day.

A company cannot build a factory big enough that all production can be carried out in one shift. One reason is that the investment per employee ranges up to $100,000 for plant and machinery. This means that if the company built a factory three times as large, the capital investment would be three times as large, and cost of the product might be three times as large. The second reason is there is a certain start-up time needed for all production. This start-up time varies with the type of material being processed. This means that the machines and material have to be warmed up to a certain temperature before the production can start flowing. One can realize that with metals, the length of time needed to warm the material to a workable condition takes a considerable time. A similar period is needed to shut down an operation. So, to minimize the start-up and shut-down time needed in a factory, the plant runs almost continuously several days a week rather than starting up and shutting down every day.

To further complicate the communications process, the typical employee is a commuter. In some states it is not unusual for a commuter to travel in excess of 60 miles daily to his job. Nor do the commuters all live in the same suburb. Some may cross state lines, some live on farms, and the factory may find its commuters living in almost a hundred different municipalities.

This means the employees don't all listen to the same radio stations, read the same newspapers, watch the same television stations.

Hence, the only feasible common means of communicating with this diverse group is by a company publication, preferably mailed to their homes.

Bigness and diversity are a way of life not only in America, but worldwide. Size and diversity are not a result of a sinister plot on the part of evil persons.

The fact is, there are jobs which cannot be performed by the home workshop. For instance, who would maintain that a backyard foundry could produce the steel needed to erect the Golden Gate Bridge or the Empire State Building?

Andrew Carnegie marveled that two pounds of iron ore, one and one-half pounds of coal, one-half pound of lime, and a small amount of manganese could be mined, transported to Pittsburgh, "and these four pounds of materials manufactured into one pound of steel, for which the consumer pays one cent."

The advantages bigness provides to the consumer are likewise evident in the case of today's automobile. It has been estimated that it would cost $50,000 if a person were to manufacture his own in a backyard shop.

The source of an organization's strength lies in bringing together a large number of persons and focusing their energies upon a single goal. But then a problem arises of how to maintain the identity and recognize the contributions of the individual in a world which increasingly must turn to the group or organization to get things done.

The organization has a great problem in melding the diverse mass of individuals of which it is composed into a cohesive team which will work for the achievement of the organization's goals.

The cooperation of these individuals is voluntary and depends upon their willingness to serve the group goals. This means that successful leadership must keep in tune with the rank and file and persuade the individuals that their success depends upon the success of the organization. Failure to do this can lead to lukewarm acceptance of the organization by the workers, poor morale, absenteeism, poor production, and eventually extinction of the organization.

Maintaining harmony between employees and organization requires that the organization communicate to the employees. The company should tell the employees:

1. What the company is doing.
2. Why the company is doing it.
3. How this will affect the employees.

Unless the organization communicates its plans and goals, it is in deep trouble.

Publications, no matter what they are called--house organ, company publication, house journal, house magazine, company newspaper--are one means by which an organization can inform its publics and thus overcome the communications problems created by its physical size.

Such a communications program will include other media, such as face-to-face meetings with supervisors, bulletin boards, letters to stockholders, letters to employees, visual aids, slides, institutional advertising, paycheck messages, customer billing messages, motion pictures, outdoor advertising, meetings, and many other devices.

Thus, before the organization goes into a communications program, and especially before the establishment of a house publication, the need to communicate should be established.

At least these questions should be answered to the full satisfaction of management:

1. Why are we planning to communicate?

2. What shall we communicate?

3. To what groups shall we communicate?

4. What will the program cost?

5. What benefits can we expect?

6. What are the limitations, or what things cannot be accomplished by communicating?

7. How extensive a program can we afford?

After management has answered all of these questions and more, if the decision is made to institute or expand a communications program, the organization should hire a professional, give him adequate budget and staff, and work with him in implementing the program.

LOST IN THE CROWD

"They (the company) don't know I exist. They never tell us anything."

These are common complaints by employees of large organizations, whether the organization is engaged in industry, religion, education, labor, or the military.

Whenever there are large aggregations of persons associated in an enterprise, communications break down. In a simpler agrarian America, people knew their neighbors. The usual organization was small and, with few persons involved, communication was direct. The employee felt real involvement with the organization. The goals of the organization were his goals. The person could see an immediate relationship between the quality of his work and customer acceptance of the product. Even further, the worker had a personal identification with the boss, and with the product. The worker was personally acquainted with the boss. Worker and employer often attended the same church on Sunday, shopped in the same stores, belonged to the same lodge, attended the same band concerts on Saturday nights.

The workman was acquainted with the product from start to finish. This meant full identification with the product and pride of accomplishment.

Now change this picture from agrarian craft industry to late twentieth-century America of the multi-national corporation. Instead of the employee's knowing his boss on a first-name basis, there has been added layer after layer of ascending steps of management—a hierarchy whose ultimate head is an almost mythical being headquartered in an office sometimes half a world away.

The product on which the craftsman formerly lavished his personal skill from start to finish has become an assembly-line product on which the workman contributes one tiny bit to the total. This contribution can be the tightening of a few screws on the right front fender of an automobile—a repetitious and boring job.

The contrast between the two life situations is the reason many persons yearn at times for a return to the simpler life of an earlier day.

But there can be no mass return to a simple agrarian culture for the simple reason that the costs of goods would be prohibitively high. People the world over demand consumer goods in great quantities, produced cheaply. To produce goods in the quantity demanded, they must be produced on an assembly-line basis at a very low per-unit cost.

This means that people must learn to live in an age of ever greater specialization, in which the problems of communications become ever more complex.

The problem, then, is how does management communicate to the individual in an organization of thousands of employees, spread over several continents, speaking many languages?

Communicating face to face, which is best, is not perfect. Communicating through a third person compounds the imperfection. When the same message is sent through a chain of command of dozens or hundreds, the message oftentimes can become badly garbled or totally lost.

Overwhelmed by the difficulty of communicating, some managers take the attitude of "Tell 'em nothing." When there is no communication downward, there is even less communication upward. When this happens, the organization is in for real trouble.

The problem is multiplied by the fact that the individual member of the organization often feels he has no one to whom he can tell his fears and frustrations. His supervisor sometimes is too busy to listen to imagined (or real) problems when the supervisor has so many problems to solve during the course of the day. The supervisor, in turn, has problems which his boss is too busy to talk about, and so on up the chain of command.

This aspect of bigness and impersonalization in organizations is probably the sole reason why white-collar employees--including teachers and creative persons, such as newspaper reporters--are joining unions.

A former assumption was that white-collar workers, supervisors, foremen, clerks, etc., automatically considered themselves professionals and identified themselves with management. This is true because the white-collar worker seems to have a natural distaste for unionization. Companies, however, have often failed to take full advantage of this situation for various reasons.

For one thing, managements sometimes overlook the white-collar worker in the decision-making process. In some cases, the first time the white-collar worker learns of a new development concerning his working situation is when the decision has already been made. There is little if any prior consultation with the lower echelons in the planning stages, in some companies. It can happen that the white-collar worker learns that management considers him to be back in the ranks, and his only function is to follow orders handed down from on high. In this case, attempts to submit ideas through the channels are snubbed, and the originator of the idea is put down by someone in the hierarchy.

A corollary development has been a lowering of wages paid white-collar workers, compared to those paid production workers. In an earlier day, the production employee was paid a meager wage and endured sometimes miserable working conditions. The white-collar worker, on the other hand, received a comparatively good wage and enjoyed relatively better working conditions.

Increasingly, under unionization, the production employee has found his wages improving in comparison with white-collar wages; in fact, white-collar wages in production industry have for some jobs dropped below those paid to production employees. This is especially so of wages paid to beginning white-collar employees, as opposed

14

to beginning production employees. The author knows of at least one instance in which production employees received more money in wages during a year than the manager of a large production factory.

These two factors--falling comparative wages and neglect by management--have created a climate in which some white-collar workers are willing to forget their anti-union bias and join a union. Unions have demonstrated ability to do two things:

1. Act as voices for their members, to guard against unfair or capricious treatment.
2. Secure their members increasingly higher wages and fringe benefits.

A further factor in the alienation of the white-collar worker from management has been an increase in working hours and pressures on the salaried employees.

The salaried employee, especially in production supervision, finds his working day significantly longer than that of the union-ized production employee. The supervisor usually must arrive at his work station several minutes ahead of the start of the shift in order to be briefed concerning the current situation. During the shift the supervisor must carry out the edicts of management and see that his charges are doing their jobs in the prescribed manner. In doing this, the supervisor faces the possibility that the union steward will engage him in discussion concerning alleged mistreat-ment of an employee or air some complaint concerning alleged poor working conditions. At the end of the shift the supervisor has to brief his incoming counterpart on the current situation in the department. Possibly the supervisor's boss may want to have a meeting to discuss safety, quality, discipline, etc. Before the supervisor leaves for home he usually must fill out some reports concerning production, quality, safety, etc.

Frequently, the supervisor carries his worries with him and continues the thinking and planning process on the way home. Often, he will take work home, or reading matter to help him become a better employee.

Because of these factors--more pressures, a longer working day, less pay--the supervisor many times decides to move back into a production job. Thus, companies lose significant numbers of potential management persons.

The situation exists that organizations can become filled with dissatisfied white-collar workers who, being trapped in their jobs, develop attitudes of cynicism toward the organization and become inefficient workers as well as outspoken critics of their company. When a company reaches this stage, the white-collar workers are ripe for unionization and it is probably too late for management to try to communicate with them.

An organization, to be successful, must be able to communicate to its employees--salaried and production--and other publics. Management must evince interest in the individual to motivate him. The organization must seek willing dedication on the part of the employees, whatever their jobs. Ideally, every employee should do his job feeling that he has a personal responsibility for the results of the company.

Too many times, the company has failed to instill this attitude in the employees. To the contrary, many a white-collar worker, even in public relations, can cite examples of management persons almost going out of their way to throw cold water on what enthusiasm the individual might have for the company. It becomes apparent that some top echelons try to stifle creativity and enthusiasm on the part of employees.

Some corporations stifle esprit de corps by basing advancement on nepotism or friendship. Some develop a regional bias, others a religious bias, some an ethnic bias. Some develop a bias against professionalism or creativity.

The developing of employee enthusiasm for the organization is not easily established nor retained. The enthusiastic employee quite obviously gets something more from his job than wages. His extra reward is the psychic income frequently mentioned by psychologists. It is the satisfaction of being treated as an important element of the organization rather than just another hired hand. This means the employee needs evidence that the organization respects him as a person who is making a significant contribution to the operations of the company.

The desire for personal status extends far upward into an organization. The author has found even plant managers, division managers, and district managers have evinced resentment at being slighted by superiors who have failed to communicate with them on some matter of organization business or operations.

On the other hand, the boss usually does not go out of his way to slight the persons he supervises. When the author at one time pointed out to a supervisor the feelings of resentment on the part of a supposedly snubbed employee, the supervisor was apologetic but puzzled. There had been no intended snub. The supervisor, overly busy with the myriad of detail to be handled day to day, admitted that he probably did not take enough time to communicate. The supervisor also pointed out that he already was spending upwards of 12 hours daily on company business, and was disinclined to increase the amount of time he spent on company matters.

The basic problem is that as organizations become large and complex, the accomplishing of simple tasks becomes complex and time-consuming. The task which in the past could have been accomplished with one visit or phone call now involves clearances from above, a proliferation of phone calls, written memorandums, committee meetings, and follow-ups to see that the assigned tasks are carried out.

It is because of the complexity of the large organizations that communications can no longer be left to each individual manager or owner. These individuals have neither the time, inclination, nor training to handle the job.

Therefore, large organizations are forced to delegate the communications function, externally and internally, to a great extent to a person or persons trained in two-way communications.

The trained communicator must be increasingly sophisticated in order to pose messages through many media, including the house journal, but should not exclude others, such as electronics, letters, bulletin boards, blimps, etc.

The organization should not jump into a communications program without making a thorough study of objectives. It would be best for the organization, even with an ongoing program of communications, to review its needs on the top management level, with the aid of a top public relations counseling firm, before a decision is made to set in motion or revise a communications program.

Chapter

3

STEPS IN PERSUASION

"He who complies against his will is of the same opinion still" (Samuel Butler). Or, as the American vernacular puts it: you can make me do it, but you can't make me like it.

Economists are fond of saying there are two means of persuasion--the carrot and the stick, or reward and punishment.

Many persons, however, have an intuitive feeling that human motivation and persuasion of that motivation are more subtle and complicated than merely reward and punishment.

Almost everyone can cite instances in which persons will do things without hope of reward, and/or in spite of threats of punishment.

Human motivation, the engineering of consent, the ability to persuade, the mystery of the mind--these are subjects with which the public relations practitioner should have considerable acquaintance. After all, an organization is not going to hire a professional communicator to disseminate information through a house journal or other means, just because he is a nice guy, or an administrator thinks it would be nice to have a house publication that looks as fancy as the one put out by a competitor. The organization is not going to do this if it has its head on straight.

Granted, there are organizations which do start a communications program with no clear idea of why. This is known as keeping up with the Joneses. Oftentimes smaller organizations of a low level of sophistication will decide to start a house journal during comparatively lush financial times for no better reason than "lots of other companies are doing it, so it must be good."

Such an ill-conceived publication may be edited by one of the office secretaries "in her spare time," or the job may be wished off on the personnel manager or some other manager. Whoever gets the job usually has no more conception of the potential or demands of the position than does the manager who made the snap decision to start the publication.

It can be predicted that, at the first signs of falling profits, the publication will be discontinued for economy reasons.

Publications, and communications programs, are instruments of persuasion; they are means of propagating the organization, in the true meaning of the word "propaganda." The birth of propaganda came in 1622 when the Roman Catholic Church under Pope Gregory XV established a committee for the "propagation of the faith." The object was to win converts and persuade mankind of "the truths of Church doctrine."

Men have been involved in trying to persuade their fellowmen from the time mankind originated, apparently. Intuitively, the author would say that it is inherent in animal nature to try to persuade. Any dog or cat owner can tell you that his pet has re-markable powers of persuasion. Dogs, especially, can be eloquent pleaders, even when they do not bark or whine.

How much more persuasive, then, can mankind be when there are added the elements of a large brain, the sophistication of language, the shrewdness of experience, and all the subtleties of psychology, electronic media, staging, etc.

Persuasion has been used, and used and used--by Moses, who persuaded the Israelites to leave Egypt and roam the deserts for 40 years; by Napoleon, who persuaded men of non-French background to fight for a French empire; by Samuel Adams, who persuaded Eng-lish Colonists to revolt; by Winston Churchill, who persuaded a defeated England to fight on against the Hitler Empire.

Persuasion also is the reason for being for a college alumni magazine, the Journal of the American Medical Association, or the employee publication of any company.

The author has heard naive statements by editors of publica-tions that said editors were maintaining objectivity in their pub-lications. The author has even heard editors of company journals complain that said editors' companies were trying to stifle objec-tivity in the publication.

The company editor who thinks his journal should be objective has to be incredibly naive. There is an old proverb, "He who pays the piper calls the tune." The organization publication, along with the entire communications program, is subjective. Objectivity is the aim of the public media: newspapers, radio, television, magazines.

The company editor should have no qualms about using persuasion in his publication, provided that he believes in the company and feels that its program deserves the goodwill and support of the community. In other words, if the company or organization is motivated to uphold the best interests of the people, the editor should have no compunction about lending his persuasive powers to selling the company's programs to the publics.

Obviously, persuasion can be bad as well as good. This all depends upon the motives of the organization and the methods used to sell its ideas, goods, or services. The persuasion of a Hitler Germany, of a Communist Russia, which distorts the truth, deals in lies, subjugates nations, or propagates irresponsible movements, is "bad."

There are persuaders of all stripe--some charlatans and rogues, some dedicated, public-spirited citizens--most somewhere in between.

Persuasion is "good" if put to good purposes, but "bad" if put to bad purposes.

It is up to the editor or communicator to decide, with his conscience as his guide, whether the organization's motives are "good" or "bad." If the communicator cannot live with himself and still "sell" the organization's program, then he should not join the organization; or upon belatedly learning that he is working for an organization whose program he cannot countenance, he should find other employment.

Communications programs will vary from organization to organization and from year to year. For example, one might say that 20 years ago the typical company employee publication was concerned mainly with establishing esprit de corps among the employees. The attempt seemed to be to establish an ingroup feeling among employees, similar to the feeling existing among the residents of a small town or city. This is one reason a goodly percentage of editors hired at that time were recruited from the reportorial staffs of small-town newspapers. The house journal then tried to recreate the intimate, newsy style of the small-town newspaper, with the company message added in various subtle or unsubtle ways.

The current organizational publications are putting great stress on community commitment and awareness. Much emphasis is being put on community involvement, problems of minority jobs and justice, pollution and its abatement, youth alienation, housing, and others.

In spite of this shift in emphasis, the underlying theme remains, as it should, to help the individual identify himself with the organization and take pride in its achievements. Any organization is in trouble when its employees or members no longer are proud of the organization and their association with it. A corollary function of the house journal and the entire communications program is to gain member support for the organization's goals and objectives.

For example, a factory would want employees to strive for a quality product, reduce waste, work safely, and produce efficiently.

A church would promote giving, attendance, good works, etc.

Whatever the organization, it must have specific goals for the publication. The organization also must take into account the elements of persuasion. The first of these is a climate of mutual trust between company and employee. No amount of sweet-talk in a publication is going to persuade employees that management is dealing fairly if the employees are convinced to the contrary.

For example, if a factory pays the lowest wages in the industry, no amount of sugarcoating the message in the employee journal will convince employees they are well paid.

In order to be persuasive, the message has to be attuned to the emotional bent of the audience as well as fitting into the frame of reference.

Changes of basic attitudes take place slowly over a very long period of time, everything else being equal. However, the change in attitude can be hastened if there is a drastic change in the frame of reference.

For example, in 1929, when the nation enjoyed bursting prosperity, the typical citizen probably was opposed to government interference with business, public tax money for relief, and social security.

However, in the mid-1930s, with the country in the depths of a depression, millions out of work and starving, the average citizen was much more willing for government to get involved in the private sector. People were glad to have government create jobs for the unemployed, spend massive amounts of tax money for relief, and supplement private pensions with social security. The frame of reference had been changed violently.

A climate of confidence, of course, depends heavily on whether or not the audience believes the source to be credible.

In 1943, Kate Smith, a singer, obtained $39 million in War Bond pledges in a 16-hour marathon appearance over radio. The listeners believed Kate Smith; so, when she asked them to buy bonds, they bought.

Lyndon Baines Johnson, on the other hand, developed a widening credibility gap in the 1960s. Johnson's loss of credibility was so great that in 1969 he announced he would not try to win re-election as President of the United States.

Fortunately for organizations, there is considerable evidence that management in general is considered a highly credible source of information by employees. This was ascertained by Opinion Research Corporation in a study carried out in 1947.

The author confirmed these findings when he carried out a survey to ascertain readership of the employee publication of the Firestone factory in Des Moines, Iowa.

To summarize, an individual or organization with a reputation for integrity and truthfulness is credible. This reputation is easy to lose if the person or organization shows signs of becoming untruthful or unethical. A recent example is the immediate reaction of letter writers, to the Akron Beacon-Journal, showing mistrust of and hostility to Jack Anderson, columnist, after Anderson admitted that he had made false accusations on a nation-

wide television show against Thomas Eagleton, running mate of George
McGovern, the 1972 Democratic presidential candidate. Anderson had
claimed he had documented proof that Eagleton had been arrested
frequently for drunken driving. Anderson later admitted, reluctantly, that the charges were without foundation.

A company which decides to communicate must define the audience which it desires to reach. In a small organization there might
be enough homogeneity of interest so that one publication would be
interesting to all. In a large company, however, there will be a
tremendous variety and range of interest and ability.

There will be highly trained engineers, accountants, comptrol-
lers, research people, and others; there will be salesmen, production employees, customers, franchised dealers, and other categories
of publics.

It is not reasonable to suppose that one publication is going
to reach and sell all of these audiences. In this case, it is wise
for the organization to decide which groups or publics it desires
and can afford to reach. Then, if a publication is in order, one
should be tailored specifically for each audience.

A publication tailored for employees would stress employee
benefits, quality, safety, etc.

A publication tailored for salesmen would concentrate on tips
to help the salesmen move the merchandise, sales contests, information about the product which would help in the sales pitch, etc.
The salesmen would not be helped by stories about fringe benefits
at the production plant any more than the production employees

would be helped by or interested in the pricing schedule for a new line of merchandise.

A publication tailored for stockholders would deal with earnings reports, dividends, and programs to make the company more profitable, and thus increase earnings and dividends.

Regardless of the number of publications produced, the editors should keep in mind that these are instruments of management. Each publication is designed to inform readers of company policy, progress, and plans for the future, also in what ways such company programs are going to affect the readers. A corollary is to solicit the readers' support in carrying out the company programs. This should be done by showing the readers how the company programs are going to help them.

It is important for management to know the effectiveness of the publication(s) or communications program. For this reason there should be periodic surveys. Such surveys should not be concerned with the comparative popularity of one feature as opposed to another. It is more significant to know how effectively the publication is communicating the company message to the readers.

This is not to say the publication should consist of dull management sermons; to the contrary, the editor should make the messages so lively and attractive that the readers want to read the publication in preference to competing leisure time activities.

In doing this, the communicator would do well to heed the words of a popular song, "Just a spoonful of sugar makes the medicine go down, in a most delightful way."

Chapter

4

SETTING THE GOALS

When Christopher Columbus sailed into the unknown western seas in 1492 he wanted to reach India by sailing west. He did not attain that goal because the American continents lay between Spain and India. Actually, Columbus did not know where he was going; and this is typical of a significant number of house journal editors. Sadly enough, many house publications don't have goals or objectives. It sometimes happens that when there are goals, they are as ill-defined or misdirected as those of Columbus.

The author in the past has polled editors at random and discovered that goals oftentimes were non-existent or very poorly defined. A typical statement by company editors seems to be that the goals are "understood but not written down."

The author once encountered a classic example of lack of goals by a company while being interviewed for a job as head of the organization's public relations. The company was unhappy with the lack of results by the public relations director.

During the course of the interview, the author asked an executive what were the areas of responsibility. A consultation with

31

other company executives disclosed that no one really knew what responsibilities the public relations director was supposed to be carrying out.

Here was a fairly large organization which had no goals for the public relations and publications programs. Just like Columbus, they did not know where they were going or how to get there.

Obviously, since the organization did not know what the public relations director was supposed to be doing, there was no way the officials could judge his effectiveness. No wonder the company was unhappy with his performance. This author never met the man, but he would guess the man was unhappy with the company.

The point is that in any enterprise, there should be firmly established goals or objectives. These goals should be established on a top-management level, and they should be written down so they can be referred to.

This does not mean that goals should be immortal, but they should be revised to meet changing conditions. However, the revisions should be made only after careful study and, again, the revisions should be done by top management. This guarantees that management is well aware of the importance of the operation. Otherwise, management may deem the program to be of little importance or frivolous and, so, unneeded. Programs which are deemed unneeded, or those which do not enjoy management esteem are the first to be cut in financial crises.

The goals or objectives should not be too narrow. The publication should not be so parochial that it ignores the company's situation as just one unit in the business community. After all, laws, taxes, and the economic climate of the entire nation are going to affect all business. Likewise, the company should keep aware of what the competition is doing, for how can the competition be opposed effectively if the organization lives in ignorance of the opponents. Football coaches constantly scout the opposition. Businesses should do the same.

On the other hand, objectives should not be too broad. Especially to be avoided is any implication that the organization is prying into or trying to regulate the private lives of employees or members.

Granted that the individual must live under the guidelines of the company with which he is affiliated; still, he has not sold his soul to that organization.

An employee must be willing to accept specific working hours, work rules, and safety regulations as part of the working conditions.

By the same token, it is not interfering in a person's private life to suggest that he drive safely, stay sober on the job, support charity, volunteer for community work, or use a seat belt.

It _is_ interfering to suggest that a person get married, attend a specific church every Sunday, donate to a specific cause, spend his leisure time in a specified manner, etc.

If the publication appears to be interfering in the employees' private lives, it runs the risk of antagonizing the readers; if it ranges too far afield from subjects of legitimate company interest, it causes them to lose interest.

Additionally, the editor must take great care to edit with restraint, or to make sure the message is subtle. The publication should be in the position of acting rather than reacting.

Take the situation where there has been an attack on the company by the union. The cause of enlightenment will not be served if the publication meets attack with attack, charge with counter-charge, name-calling with name-calling.

The company publication must maintain a low-key tone in its communications. An even-tenored, reasoned approach to its subjects will serve the situation better than if the editor allows his temper to show through in his writings. Readers will be much more impressed by words which reflect sweet reasonableness than by ill-tempered rantings. The British, who are excellent propagandists, used this approach with great success during World War II. As a result, the people of Europe listened to the British Broadcasting Company to learn the "truth" rather than listening to the shrill rantings of the German propaganda broadcasts. The BBC was factual and maintained an air of calm and reasonableness in its broadcasts. It is the author's impression that few people respect the person who shouts or descends to invective, whether the person is a friend, relative, or editor.

Not only should the message be subtle, meaning that it should be couched in a low key and stated calmly, but the message is much more effective if it is stated by the reader's peers rather than top management. This is not to say the editor should never carry messages directly from management. Of course there should be direct communication from management, fully identified as such.

However, such communication should be kept within reason so the readers do not tune out or feel that management is forever preaching to them.   1965827

For effective persuasion, the editor should put the company message in the employees' words. For example, on the question of quality for a production company, the editor might try the following approach for his stories. He could locate an employee who has a good record of quality production and write a story about him, having him tell of the importance of producing a quality product. Also, the editor could have the employee tell what he does on the job to assure quality production. This same principle is equally effective for most of the stories in which the editor tries to persuade.

A further caution is for the editor to act rather than react. This means the editor should constantly discuss the publication with key executives to see what stories are needed to prepare the audience for changes or programs which are to go into effect several months or years later. Putting out fires after they start should be avoided. The editor should work from an affirmative angle by discovering the problem areas before they become problems. By publishing material about a potential problem, he might defuse a possible explosion.

In order to persuade, the story must be told and retold many, many times, in an almost infinite variety of ways. Persons seldom absorb a message on the first telling; oftentimes the message is still obscure on the second telling. Additionally, basic attitudes toward issues are changed only very slowly, and then after the subject has been told many times.

It should be remembered that in all of the telling and retelling of stories, the materials should fit in with the objectives of the publication.

Although the goals of each publication should be tailored to fit the need of the organization, an editor can get some good ideas for setting up the objectives for his publication by studying the goals of another one. Here, for example, are some areas in which production companies are usually concerned; so an editor might use as part of his goals the printing of stories concerning:

1. Employee recognition
2. Safety
3. Suggestions
4. Quality
5. Giving blood
6. Environment
7. Minority hiring
8. Financial situation
9. Waste control
10. Production milestones
11. Bond sales
12. Industry news
13. New products

The list, of course, would have to conform to the needs of the organization. The organization would have to decide the frequency with which each type of story should appear in the publication.

Chapter

5

METHODS OF PERSUASION

The publisher of a country weekly was trying to sell a merchant an advertisement for the coming week's paper.

"I don't believe I need to advertise any longer," said the merchant. "After all, I have been at this location 10 years now; so all the customers know me."

"How long," countered the publisher, "has the church been on the hill?"

"Oh, about a hundred years, I guess," replied the merchant. "Why do you ask?"

"Well," answered the publisher, "don't they still ring the bell on Sundays?"

The merchant bought the ad.

Repetition is the basis of all persuasion. It is a process of learning, relearning, and reinforcing. Just as it is not enough for a man to tell his wife once that he loves her, the message should be repeated frequently and in an infinite variety of ways.

So it is with the communicator; the company message must be reiterated constantly or it fails to get across.

Learning is by repetition, and the house journal is a teaching device. It teaches the audience the company message, whether it is directed toward salesmen, employees, dealers, the general public, or some other group.

Pavlov demonstrated this principle very convincingly with his dogs. He experimented by ringing a bell just before he fed the animals. After many times of doing this, it got so that every time the bell rang, the dogs would salivate. This is known as a conditioned reflex.

Now, a communicator probably cannot condition his audience to the extent that Pavlov did his dogs. However, the principle is the same. It takes constant repetition to sell an idea.

Why is this?

In the first place, persons seldom absorb much of a message on the first telling. Oftentimes, the message still is not totally clear on the second or even third telling.

Added to this is the fact that it takes a long time to change basic attitudes; it should be kept in mind that the message might run counter to the reader's upbringing, experience, or biases. This is the reason why it is best to have the message come from the reader's peer group.

Secondly, the reader might skip over the message the first time it appears; so the editor hopes the reader will see it the second time around, or the third, or on a later telling.

Readers are busy and have a lot of demands on their leisure time, so the reader might not even see a given issue of the publi-

cation. Additionally, through a flaw in the distribution system,
the reader might not even receive a given issue.

Also, the audience is constantly changing. In some organizations, turnover is fantastically high--30 percent or higher yearly.
One of the author's company editor friends is required to use a
picture of each new employee. The problem is that most of the employees are girls just graduated from high school. Within a year,
a high percentage of the girls have married and left the company.
Sometimes the new employee has left the company within a week of
being hired and before her picture appears in the publication.

Because there is a high turnover in the reading audience, repetition of the company message becomes even more important. If
there is a turnover of 25 percent yearly, this means one-fourth of
this year's audience didn't read the company message printed last
year.

In being repetitive, the communicator must be sure to vary the
approach so the readers do not tune out the message. The communicator should be as subtle as a skilled chef who can prepare one food
in a great variety of ways--eggs fried, eggs boiled, eggs poached,
eggs scrambled, eggs Benedict, shirred eggs, eggs in omelets, etc.

The editor can present his ideas, using the same principle--
safety in cartoons, safety from management's viewpoint, safety as
an inquiring reporter feature, safety awards, safety-slogan contests, "why I work safely" stories featuring employees with superi-
or safety records, editorials about safety, pictures about new safety devices, etc.

A corollary is telling the story to show how the subject affects the individual reader, for this is one of the things the readers want to know about the organization--what does all of this mean to me. From time to time the editor can overtly caption a story, in effect, "what this means to you." However, it is not good to overdo this device, or the readers, again, may tune out.

In writing persuasive communications it is necessary to motivate the readers through making the writing live. This fact has been pointed out by both Rudolph Flesch and Robert Gunning in their books which advocate simplification of writing.

The writing is more effective if the sentences, paragraphs, and words are shorter. Along the same lines, the writing must be in the reader's frame of reference--put in terms with which he is familiar.

Here is an example of how the editor can express things in terms familiar to the reader or make the writing vivid: One of the Firestone tire factories had the engineers figure out that, if one day's production of passenger car tires were stacked tire on tire, the resulting pile would stand $12\frac{1}{2}$ times as high as the Empire State Building.

Almost any large organization uses impressive amounts of water and electricity. The editor can compare the amount of water used by the factory to the amount used by a city of a specific population. For example, he can say his factory uses enough water to supply a city of 20,000, if the engineers say this is so. There is a tremendous potential in most companies for making similar comparisons, so the editor puts the facts in terms the reader can grasp easily. (In this day of concern for the environment, it might be best not to put too much emphasis upon the usage rate of scarce natural resources.)

Not only must the material be lively and personal, but there must be some validity in the minds of the readers. The writer must tell the reader his authority for the statements made in writing.

For example, if there is an article in the publication on the subject of economics and there is no authority quoted, the story becomes much less believable. Or, if the writer cites the opinions of someone who is not qualified, the story carries little weight with the reader. In order for the communicator to gain the confidence of the readers, he must cite a qualified expert in the field.

Of course, the writing must be lucid, grammar must represent good usage, syntax must be correct, punctuation must be standard, and copyreading and proofreading must be as nearly perfect as humanly possible.

Above all, writer and editor must be able to keep the facts straight. Stories should answer all the questions which arise in the minds of the readers. In other words, the writers must be trained writers, with considerable competence in their trade.

If the writers and editors are careless or sloppy, the readers give little heed to the communication. Surprisingly, there are some company publications which are poorly written and edited. It is the author's opinion that the reader is insulted by such a publication and, therefore, thinks less of the organization for producing a shoddy one. If the organization cannot or will not produce a well-written and -edited publication, the organization would do better to produce nothing. It would be better in this case to confine written communications to letters from the president.

Chapter

6

PUBLICATION STRENGTHS AND WEAKNESSES

Nothing succeeds like success. However, the other side of the coin is that success in one field does not necessarily guarantee success in another.

In the early stages of World War II, The Maytag Company of Newton, Iowa, started an employee publication, the <u>Maytag Bulletin</u>, for the sole purpose of selling War Bonds to the employees. The medium was an immediate spectacular success. In fact, the publication was such a success in this endeavor that Maytag kept it as a means of selling other management goals. Management soon discovered, however, that other goals were less easy to sell than the War Bonds.

Maytag management learned, as have so many others, that the house journal has limitations on what it can do.

But why is this? If a publication can sell War Bonds to employees, why can't it achieve the same level of success at selling safety, for example?

Well, for this simple reason--that in order to be effective the message must be attuned to the mental and emotional climate of the receiver. The recipient of the message must be receptive to the message; it must not violate his sense of fitness, it must conform to his frame of reference.

It must not be contrary to what he has learned all of his life as being right, natural, and true. It cannot violate his code of ethics, his fabric of ethical and moral standards. Even more, the message must be vivid, it must relate directly to him, it must show in the simplest terms a course of action with which he agrees.

The War Bonds issue fits in almost totally with all criteria. Buying Bonds was patriotic. The money would be used to help defend the country and support our brave boys fighting overseas against an enemy which had treacherously attacked us. Buying Bonds was a way in which the employee could sacrifice, in some small measure, in lieu of engaging in personal combat with the enemy. Even though the purchaser did sacrifice, in the nature of saving money instead of spending it for immediate gratification of needs or pleasures, the money was not lost. Additionally, the sacrifice asked was not one which could be interpreted as helping the company.

The issue, then, was clearly a simple one which was heavily in tune with the emotional bent of the audience. Again, the action desired by the Maytag Bulletin was simple--buying Bonds.

On the other hand, almost any other message the company would try to sell would be more complicated, such as the issue of working safely.

Such an issue is a fairly hazy, ill-defined concept. In the first place, the individual does not think that accidents can happen to him. In the second place, the employee does not think that safety is his concern, but should rightly be the concern of the company. The company should provide clean, comfortable, safe working conditions. Not only that, but, in the thinking of many employees, the installation of safety devices on machines, the institution of safety rules, the required use of personal safety equipment--all are merely harassment on the part of the company.

Almost any industrial safety director can cite instances in which employees will find ways to bypass safety devices on dangerous machines.

The author has seen many instances in which the operator of a powerful press would wire down the dead-man switch so that he could operate the machine faster. The dead-man switch will prevent the machine from operating unless it is depressed. The device is designed to keep the operator from putting his hands into the machine while it is in operation.

There also is formidable resistance by employees to wearing such devices as safety glasses, safety shoes, safety gloves, etc. The employees will complain that safety glasses hurt their ears or noses; they will complain that safety shoes hurt their feet; they will complain that goggles get dusty and they can't see through them, or that goggles are hot or impede their work, etc.

For these reasons, the selling of a company concept such as employee safety becomes a complicated issue. Employee motivation is not clear-cut; the employee is not emotionally charged to support safety. Any gain, in the mind of the employee, is a gain for the company.

The issue is not clear-cut, the employee is not emotionally motivated, there is no readily defined goal, the employee is not pre-sold on the program, and there is no quickly gained, valuable reward.

For these and other reasons, the programs which the organization tries to sell through the publication must be sold over a long period of time.

Some programs cannot be sold at all. For instance, the publication cannot solve organizational problems, such as company-union friction, nor can the publication reverse employee hostility to a company program. For instance, if food in the company cafeteria is inferior, no amount of rationalization in the house journal is going to convince employees to the contrary. The company will have to take positive action which will improve the food.

It takes a long time to sell an idea through the company publication. The publication must present the problem of employee safety, for instance, over a period of many issues, before the editor can hope to start getting the message across.

Additionally, the publication cannot divorce the individual from his natural loyalty to a group. For example, if the individual is a member of a union, the publication message is not going to divorce him from his loyalty to the union program. Of course, there will be a few exceptions, but these exceptions are not significant. Oftentimes an individual is going to support his group's program against those whom he considers to be outsiders, despite the fact he might not necessarily think the program is the best. In the same manner, the overwhelming majority of members of a political party will vote for the party's candidates and platform despite the members' feeling that another party might have a slightly superior platform and/or candidates.

Another thing a publication cannot do is consistently offer concrete examples of accomplishments. Once in a great while a publication, such as the Maytag Bulletin, can demonstrate concrete evidence that it has boosted the sales of War Bonds. Even in this case, the publication cannot make claim that it was the sole motivating factor. Maybe the War Bonds would have sold through some other medium. Additionally, there no doubt were other efforts used in selling the Bonds at Maytag, such as bulletin board notices, personal letters, radio broadcasts, etc.

The publication cannot do the job of persuasion by itself, nor should it be expected to do so.

The organization should realize that the publication is only one part of a continuing and wide-ranging program of information and persuasion. Just as a man should not stop telling his wife he loves her, so the organization should not stop communicating with its publics, either on the assumption that once sold, always sold, or on the premise that just because we can't measure results we should stop communicating. As surely as the organization stops trying to communicate, it can guarantee that its message cannot be received. If you don't talk, no one can hear you.

A corollary to these rather negative cautions concerning what a publication cannot do is some affirmative aspects of what the publication can accomplish.

The publication can transmit a message to the audience with total fidelity; that is, the message does not become garbled by going through several channels. For example, messages which are transmitted orally become distorted.

A case in point would be if a company president gave a talk to the factory managers. The factory managers would make oral transmission of that talk to the department heads, who would talk to the supervisors, who would pass it on orally to the employees. There would be successive and progressive distortion and loss of detail in each step of the transmission.

In contrast, the editor of a publication would have time to learn and transmit to the audience the entire operation of the organization. The individual supervisor, on the other hand, would probably be limited in work experience to the operations of his area.

A further plus is that the publication not only reaches the immediate recipient, but has the potential of reaching friends and family. In the case of an employee publication, this is especially important. A person might almost say that reaching the employee is a secondary goal. Granted, the avowed purpose is to reach the employee with the company message. However, the employee already knows something about the company, albeit he has a rather restricted image—and a garbled one at that. To the employee's spouse and children, the company is usually an intriguing mystery. The bread-winner disappears into the company every day for a period of time, spending probably more than half of all waking hours at the company. Because people are poor observers and communicators, the average employee transmits a rather confused, piecemeal picture to his family of the place where he works.

In other words, the employee really knows little of what goes on at his place of work and tells very little of that to the spouse and family.

A rather amusing illustration is an occurrence connected with the author's establishing a house journal for the employees of the Des Moines, Iowa, Firestone plant.

The employees had some idea that a publication was planned, but there was no full realization that one was really going to be initiated, or when it would be published.

The first issue appeared on May 1, 1953. In that initial is-sue was the story about a large suggestion award paid to a produc-tion employee in March. The morning after the issue went into the mail, this employee confronted the author.

"Are you the editor of the Hawkeye?" he asked.

"Yes; why?" I said.

"Well, you got me into a lot of hot water," he said.

"Why is that?" I said.

"Well," he replied, "you had a story that I won a big sugges-tion award. I never told my wife I won the money, and I spent it for a new boat. When I drove into the driveway last night, she ran out of the house screaming, 'What did you do with all that money?'"

"She really worked me over."

This illustrates the extent to which spouses are in ignorance of what goes on at the company and to what extent the house journal can help dispel the lack of information about that organization in the minds of the employees' families.

For this reason, it is best if the employee publication is mailed to the homes of the employees. In any situation where the organization wants to reach the entire family, it is best to mail to the home. Otherwise, there are reasons why the family does not gain access to the publication. Not the least of these reasons may be that the employee might not want the spouse to know too much about what is going on at the company.

Employees have told the author many times that their wives would put tremendous pressure on them to make suggestions to the company in hopes of supplementing their incomes. When the publication is distributed at company gates or through company mail, it is easy for the employee to keep it from his family, in case there is something in there that he doesn't want the family to know about.

Intuitively, and by the use of feedback from employees, the editor is going to "feel" whether his publication is well read.

Management, however, is not going to accept the bases of intuition or conversations in the cafeteria as real proof of readership. It is therefore necessary for the editor to obtain sound statistics concerning readability and readership of the publication. Provable statistics impress management and should impress the editor.

This means that the organization should make periodic studies of the publication audience to check for readership. In making such studies, it is best if the study is done by an agency not associated with the organization. This does not mean the study necessarily has to be done by one of the top national polling organizations.

To the contrary, almost any university has on its staff individuals who are competent researchers. Such individuals usually are glad to serve as consultants and will do readership studies for the editor. Another source would be students working on master's or on doctor's degrees. These students might be willing to do such studies for very low fees because they would be able to get college credit for doing significant independent study.

Barring these possibilities, the editor's organization might have a Ph.D. in the marketing department. Such an individual could give invaluable advice in the operation of a readership survey.

Another source of aid and advice would be the editors of other company publications. Industrial editors are almost always glad to share their expertise, so it should be comparatively easy to find one who has done a readership survey and pick his brain.

Another source is the headquarters of the International Association of Business Communicators. The director is more than happy to help members, or non-members, in sharing the organization's knowledge of industrial editing.

Readership surveys usually show that the employee publication is well read and believed. Many readers develop a fierce loyalty toward their publication, some will save every copy, and some will even have the copies bound.

Usually the publication, in its competition for the employees' leisure time comes off well. However, the publication must contain material of significance and substance, or run the danger of the audience's tuning out.

*   *   *

The author is indebted to The Maytag Company, Newton, Iowa, for permission to refer to the company publication, the Bulletin.

In citing the Bulletin, the author wants to make sure the reader does not conclude that Maytag management is naive, nor that the Bulletin is ineffective.

To the contrary, the author has long admired Maytag management for its sophistication and effectiveness, as well as the company's real concern for the customer. Also, the Bulletin is one of the nation's more effective house journals, well tailored to its audience. Maytag employees believe in their publication and in their company.

Chapter

7

WHO NEEDS A PUBLICATION?

One man's meat is another man's poison. What is a necessity for one organization becomes a luxury for another. It follows, therefore, that not every organization needs a publication. The question of whether the organization needs one can be answered only by that organization.

One of the criteria is size. Intuitively, the author would say that whenever an organization approaches 1,000 employees, dealers, etc., in numbers, it should take a close look at its communications program and assess the needs. Quite probably the managers and executives will begin to realize there is an increasing communications lag long before the company reaches this size. It is hard to communicate on a regular basis with 1,000 individuals unless there is a written periodical issued at stated intervals.

Another criterion is complexity. A large organization in which all the members are concentrated in one area might be able to handle internal communications by word of mouth. It is conceivable that a college of 1,000 persons, including faculty, staff, and students, could gather the entire membership into one meeting place at intervals and thus handle the communications problem in periodic face-to-face meetings.

On the other hand, if there is an organization of 500 persons or fewer, in which the members are stationed some distance apart, the organization probably is in need of a house journal to maintain the communications. Such an organization might be a small insurance company which would have agents in major American cities. It could be a rental or leasing organization consisting largely of one person offices in various cities.

The need for a publication must also take into account less definable criteria. For example, word-of-mouth communication is notoriously ephemeral and inaccurate.

To test this premise, following a lecture, one could ask any member of the audience to recount in detail the points made by the speaker, and the range of answers would be almost as great as the number of persons polled. Most of the audience may remember, at best, only one or two salient points. The odds are that even those remembered points will not be quite in focus in the listener's mind.

Writing is for the record. The written word can be referred to. This means that the communicator can spell out in detail the message which is to be conveyed and that message is then delivered verbatim to the audience.

Before the organization makes a decision whether to start a publication, management should make a thorough study of the question from all angles.

In seeking the answer to, "Why are we planning to publish?," management should not accept such answers as, "Because other companies this size have a publication."

Instead, the company should answer the question, "Do we have a communications gap which can be plugged by a publication?"

As indicated before, the management should consult with other organizations of similar size and nature. A thorough study should be made of the communications programs of such organizations to see if these programs might profitably be adapted.

Then the management should ascertain approximate costs and decide whether the company can afford such a program.

If, after a thorough study of all the pros and cons of publishing, the company decides there is a real need to communicate through a house journal, the company should take steps to begin a publication.

Now the organization is ready to hire an editor and, with editor and management working together, take the first step of publication, which is to prepare a list of objectives or goals.

Chapter

8

CHOOSING THE EDITOR

Time was when the large organization, typically, would recruit a small-town newspaper reporter whenever someone was needed to edit a company publication.

There were sound reasons for so doing. One reason was that the company sought to recreate through its publication the small-town camaraderie among the employees, a feeling of one for all and all for (the company) one. This is the atmosphere the reporter had worked to achieve for the small-town newspaper. To a great extent, the small-town newspaper is an extension of the business community of the town, and probably the greatest cohesive power. It is the magnet which draws the otherwise diverse residents into a whole. The small-town newspaper is dependent for the major part of its revenues upon the local merchants. They are the main advertisers.

To stay profitable, the paper helps to promote the "trade at home" theme, thus minimizing the loss of home trade to shopping centers, mail order houses, and nearby cities. The small-town newspaper also tries to sell the readers on the attractiveness of living in its particular small town in an attempt to diminish the outflow of young people.

The small-town newspaper writer learns quickly to adapt a more kindly, low-key approach to news than would be taken in a metropolitan paper. In the personal atmosphere of a small town, the news source is close to the reporter, and vice versa.

The small-town news source might come into the office and punch the reporter in the nose, if irritated at what he feels to be unjust news treatment. At the minimum, the irritated news source, and his friends and relatives, can exert pressures which would be impossible to exert in a city. For example, the social atmosphere can become suddenly very unpleasant from the presence of so many cold shoulders. Sometimes the flow of news tips can dry up to a trickle or cease altogether.

Thus, the small-town reporter often is promotion-oriented—much more so, probably, than a similar staff member on a metropolitan daily.

But the reasons go deeper than that.

On the small publication, the reporter handles all sorts of news—society, city council, courthouse, sports, and weather—plus features, editorials, and more. This means the reporter is a generalist, and not a specialist. He writes what has to be written in large quantities; therefore, he can handle almost any news assignment with a surprising degree of proficiency. Oftentimes, on stories which involve technical subjects with which the writer might not be familiar, and also with features, he will check back with the source to make sure the facts are accurate or make sense.

The country reporter has another plus going for him in that he not only can handle a wide range of subjects with comparative ease, but is fully aware of the production aspects.

He almost always has some expertise at photography, to the extent not only of taking pictures, but of developing and enlarging them. He also has some proficiency in choosing meaningful pictures to illustrate a story, in cropping the pictures, and in scaling them to size.

He can write a headline and meet a deadline. He can lay out a page and trim a story to fit the space. He knows the problems faced by the backshop. He often is aware of, and helps face, the problems of circulation, distribution, and promotion.

He sometimes deals with suppliers, sells advertising, judges beauty contests, or gives talks. Comparatively, he is a more diversified, well-rounded person than a metropolitan newsman with the same number of years' professional experience.

Now it so happens that these all are attributes which are needed by the editor of a company publication. According to studies by the International Association of Business Communicators, more than half of the members do the job alone or with the help of one other person. Not only is the typical company editor virtually a one-man band, but the same editor will find there are other related duties attached to the job. The editor accepts such auxiliary jobs almost as a matter of course, because he is used to writing a large flow of copy daily. By comparison, the amount of writing for the company publication seems, at first, to be small.

Although many organizations still would prefer to hire small-town reporters as company editors, there are several reasons why the company is forced to seek elsewhere for a source of supply.

In the case of medium-sized and large dailies, salaries have been rising to a fairly reasonable figure; so fewer reporters are leaving the newspapers. There seems to be a trend for reporters from medium-sized dailies to seek positions on metropolitan newspapers, once they have proven their writing ability, rather than seeking jobs in industrial journalism.

On the other hand, there seems to be a growing number of persons who train specifically for industrial journalism while still college students. In this way, the student gains some training in the theories of economics, business administration, marketing, public relations, and other business-oriented subjects.

Many colleges which teach industrial editing also offer classroom practice in aspects of producing a company publication.

Many professors, including the author, urge students to supplement their college training with significant experience as small-town newspaper reporters before taking jobs as company publication editors. The college graduate who does this may discover that newspapering is a more rewarding career than industrial editing.

This individual may discover he has talents as a business or trade writer and may decide on a career in business papers or trade journals. On the other hand, the same individual, after a stint of newspapering, would be more valuable to a company as publication editor. The main value of small-town newspaper experience means the individual has added depth to his background, thus increasing possible options for his future career.

The reporter who has spent a couple years as a general assignment reporter, and then has specialized as a business writer, would make an excellent house journal editor. The problem here is that a specialty writer probably can earn a large salary from his newspaper; so he might not be tempted to take a comparatively smaller salary for a job which is more confining and circumscribed.

Some organizations are beginning to show a preference for editors who have trained in college specifically for the job of industrial editor, even though the ink is still wet on the diploma and the editor has had no professional media experience. These organizations feel there is less need for the editor to have overt newspaper experience, but a greater need for training in the business-oriented subjects.

In some cases, organizations see no need for any training whatsoever for a company publication editor.

Such organizations seem to feel the job is a simple one, which is to put words down on paper. Stenographers are fast at putting words down on paper. Stenographers don't command salaries as high as persons with college degrees. Therefore, the organization might reason, we will turn the editing job over to one of the stenographers. After all, goes the reasoning, with a four-page tabloid set in eight-point type, there are 72,000 words. The author's stenographer can type at an average speed of 90 words a minute. Therefore, the girl should be able to do all the writing for the publication in 13 hours and 20 minutes, a little more than a day and a half a month. Ridiculous as it may seem, the author has heard company officials reason similarly.

What guidelines, then, should the organization follow in looking for an editor? In the first place, the organization should publish a house publication only if there is a demonstrated need to overcome a communications gap and if the company is financially able to budget such a publication.

Bearing in mind the sensitive nature of the job, the organization should hire an editor who is skilled in persuasion and judgment. As to salary, the organization should be willing to pay a wage commensurate with the editor's training and experience, and with the importance of the job. Surprisingly, organizations sometimes put the salary of the communicator at a very low level. For instance, in some concerns one can find editors who are paid much less than some production workers, although it takes many years of preparation for the editor to learn his job, while the production worker can learn the necessary assembly line skills in a matter of weeks.

Secondly, the organization should know that the publication tends to take on the personality of the editor. Therefore, the publication should make a thorough study of the individual's motivation, personality, and abilities, as well as the usual school record and three references.

The organization should realize this is not a 9:00 to 5:00, punch-the-time-card type of job. There are times when, with deadlines to meet, the editor might work far into the night or even through an entire weekend without expecting extra compensation. This means the organization should seek an editor with a singular amount of dedication to the job. The organization should be careful that, once they have hired an editor who has the necessary devotion and dedication, corporate cussedness does not turn off his enthusiasm for the job.

An editor should have the skills pertaining to producing print media: writing, editing, layout, production. The organization should refrain from loading the editor with so many details that the publication and other communication efforts are produced in an off-the-cuff manner.

The organization should seek an editor with sensitivity, one who works well with other persons, has an affirmative outlook toward life, and is insatiably curious about almost everything. This is so because, as mentioned earlier, the editor indelibly puts the stamp of his personality on the publication. If the editor is negative or unenthusiastic, those attitudes cannot help but show through in his writing. If the editor has a low level of curiosity, he will tend not to ask enough questions so there will be information gaps in his writing. By the same token, a surly disposition will mean an editor who cannot communicate effectively with persons.

Where does a company seek an editor? Many still find satis-factory replacements from the ranks of defecting newspapermen. Another growing source is the college campus, where more and more colleges are teaching some of the basics of industrial editing, feature writing, and business and economics, as well as makeup and layout, picture production, and editing.

The size of the staff should be varied with the size of the job to be done. If the editor is to produce a small tabloid news-paper monthly, probably one person can do the job if assisted by a secretary and given aid by the company photographer. If, how-ever, the organization desires to increase the frequency of pub-lication and/or the number of pages, more staff members will be needed. Management should also keep in mind that a magazine will demand more staff than a comparable-sized newspaper and take longer lead time in production.

Organizations should, if possible, avoid the trap of relying on company or plant reporters to take the place of competent as-sistants to the editor. In the first place, such reporters almost never have any training in journalism and will report the trivial and inane while overlooking material of significance. Secondly, the reporters are being asked to do the job in their spare time at no pay, except the doubtful prestige they may gain by having their names printed on the masthead.

Sophisticated organizations seem to be relying less upon the doubtful offerings of plant reporters and more upon the paid staff members of the company publication.

Once having hired an editor (and staff) for the publication, the organization should continue assisting that individual in doing his job to the utmost. The best way to do this is to show the editor that management has a sincere interest in the publication and in the editor's efforts to achieve the objectives. The editor should be constantly encouraged to make the publication fresher and more substantial. He should be continually encouraged to update his skills by attending short courses and conferences, by having memberships in professional organizations, and/or by enrolling in college or university courses related to his job. As the editor grows in understanding of the organization and business at large, the publication should reflect this growth. The editor will become an ever more valuable member of the management team.

Chapter

9

WORKING IN THE ORGANIZATION

Organizations take on complexity as they take on size. The larger the organization becomes, the more it starts to resemble the military. This is true whether the organization is a family, church, factory, or government.

As the unit becomes large, the communications between its constituent parts break down. The company tends to become sealed off into little air-tight compartments. Each compartment has a job to do and, to a certain extent, develops an ingroup state of mind. The compartment now has less loyalty to the whole than it does to the part.

The heads of these various compartments become jealous of their fiefs and prerogatives. An individual who tries to usurp any of the prerogatives of one of these compartments will find himself under instant attack. For this reason, intricate systems of conduct exist in large organizations to make sure that the parts cooperate so that the whole can operate and make a profit. Organizations become so complicated that their people sometimes say, rather facetiously, that the company makes a profit in spite of itself.

There is no map or blueprint for the company editor to follow in threading his way through the maze of company prerogatives and jealousies. The problem is complicated by the fact that the editor is one of the few individuals who tries to cut across the lines of force. He is trying to pull the parts into a cohesive whole, welding loyalty to the company; at the same time, the various parts are pulling and hauling in different directions, tending to make the whole less cohesive.

A further complication is that the very fact of starting a publication means there is created the potential for an increased workload on some of these compartments, and the affected departments will not like it.

The first thing the editor should know is that being the editor of a company publication is vastly more complicated than being the editor of a weekly or daily newspaper. The newspaper reporter writes the story in his own words, either as an eyewitness to an event or after interviewing a news source. His superior might make some minor changes in copy to avoid libel, correct misspellings, or make the material factually correct. Otherwise, the story is printed as the reporter wrote it.

The company publication may be changed several times from the time the editor writes the first draft until legal counsel finally puts an okay on the material. For the newspaper reporter, the first draft is often the final draft.

The first thing the editor must do is learn about the organi-

zation, meeting as many persons as possible before he does anything.
The most important person is the individual's immediate superior.
The editor should never hesitate to consult his immediate superior
about anything and everything. The time will come when some items
will become routine and the superior will say, "Just use your own
good judgment." However, the editor is being supervised by his
superior. The superior is assumed to know at all times exactly
what projects the editor has going, and at what stage of progress
the editor is in each project.

A very good idea is to seek the superior's advice on all matters, trivial though they may seem. The editor shouldn't stick
his boss's neck out. He should be sure his boss knows what he is
doing and has given the go-ahead to do it, especially if the project involves spending company money or using company time, material,
or personnel.

The editor must learn which person has charge of what function
in the organization and seek the aid and advice of each person who
is in a decision-making position. This means an idea must be explained and sold probably several times to several persons.

Of course, the procedure will vary from organization to organization, since each has set up operations to fit its peculiar
needs. The best guide in following company procedures is to ask
the immediate superior the specifics of operation in that company.

Here, roughly, is how ideas are sold in some organizations:
First, the editor broaches the idea to the boss. If the boss says,

go-ahead, it sounds like a good one, he advances the idea to the boss's boss and in successive steps to the head of the organization (sometimes the boss will clear the idea with the organization head). If the company head thinks the idea is good, the editor presents the idea to the company treasurer or comptroller, if it involves spending money above and beyond that already appropriated or involves taking persons off their normal jobs for an appreciable length of time. If material or service is to be purchased outside the company, he consults with the purchasing agent, whose prerogative it is to do all of the buying. Next, he consults with any persons whose departments will be involved in the proposed idea.

To get down to specifics, here is how the process will go in a working situation. We'll say that the editor, who also has public relations duties, has an idea to have a motion picture training film made.

The editor works for a tire factory. The film will be used to train new tire builders and will be shown to civic groups. Additionally, excerpts from the film will be used in company publications.

The editor outlines the idea to his boss. The boss may say, "The idea seems to have merit; how much money are we talking about?"

Because the company does not have facilities for taking or processing motion pictures, the editor must locate possible suppliers from outside. He goes to the purchasing agent and asks for a cost estimate for having a motion picture company prepare a film of the desired length.

The purchasing agent contacts two or three potential suppliers who then submit estimates of the costs, after having learned the details of the desired length of the film. The suppliers also estimate the time it will take to shoot the film on location in the factory, and the time it will take to edit the film to the desired length. The editor ascertains what is needed in the line of electrical outlets.

The editor then consults with the head of the tire-building department and ascertains the cost of tying up the builder(s) and the desired machine(s) for the time needed to shoot the film.

The editor has to estimate the cost of cleaning the area—possibly painting the machines—and probably the cost of having a janitor and an electrician on hand prior to, and during, the filming. In each case, the editor has to outline the plan to the person or persons who supervise the electrician(s) and janitor(s).

Armed with all of the facts, the editor presents the plan orally and in writing to his boss, being sure to emphasize the benefits the company will gain by the expenditure of time and money. The organization always should have a sound reason for spending money, since money does not flow in a limitless stream and the company which spends money unwisely can soon go broke.

If the boss says this is a good idea, go ahead—it usually means go ahead and sell it to the higher-ups. Oftentimes the next step is to prepare a written purchase order request on which the plan will be outlined formally, and the estimate of costs and name of the supplier noted. This request then is submitted to the necessary executives for approval after the boss has noted his approval in writing on the purchase order.

The procedures may differ from organization to organization, but the principles are the same. Of course, the larger the organization, the more formalized the procedure; the smaller the organization, the less formalized. If the organization is small enough, one verbal approval may suffice.

In due time, the purchase order request comes back either denied or with the necessary approvals. If denied, the editor files the idea for possible submission at a later time. Sometimes a good idea is deferred by management because there simply is no money available. In this case, management may suggest resubmission of the plan during the next fiscal year or at some time in the future. At any rate, the denial should be accepted with grace. It should be remembered that not even the president of the company has all of his ideas accepted.

If the idea is approved, the editor sets up a schedule, mutually satisfactory to the supplier and company, of times for the filming. It is best to check first with the head of the tire-building department to find out when the filming would be least disruptive of the work schedule. Then, the filming company is asked to do its filming within the acceptable time schedule.

With an editor, liaison, follow-up, scheduling, and planning are of paramount importance. He should remember—follow up, follow up, remind, remind, remind. He should also keep check lists of all things to be done.

These are crucial differences between the newspaper reporter and the house journal editor. The industrial editor is also a public relations practitioner. There are too many things going on to enable the editor to keep everything in memory, so he should write things down.

The industrial editor in any organization of considerable size will have to work with a system of clearances. This means that, to a varying degree, company officials will want to check the stories before they appear in the publication(s).

This is done, not because the organization distrusts the editor(s), but because the editor(s) cannot possibly be aware of the daily shifts in management thinking. Through constant checking of story material, management is continually aware that the publication is there and that it is important. Management clearance of material means management involvement in the publication.

By all means, the company's legal counsel should clear the entire publicaton before it goes to the printer. For this reason it is imperative that a specific time be established each week or month, prior to publication, when the rough dummy, containing all material to be used, should be submitted to the counsel for careful reading. If humanly possible, editor and counsel should both abide by the established schedule.

Because working in the organization can be complicated, it is worth some repetition in explaining the handling of stories. We will say, for example, the editor wants a story about a new product. Probably the place to go is to the head of research and development. We will say that this person has a new product just about ready to go on the market.

The first step is to have the department manager supply all of the facts about the product. Then there is an arrangement made to have pictures taken to illustrate the story. If the product is a large machine, the picture might feature someone operating the machine. However, the editor has to draw upon his imagination, with suggestions from a photographer, in deciding upon a proper picture to use.

An attempt should always be made to get an action photograph or one in which action is implied.

If the organization has a news bureau as well as company publication(s), the preparation of new product stories probably is the province of the news bureau. Even if there is a news bureau, the company editor keeps looking for features which the news service might have overlooked.

After interviewing the department manager, the editor writes a rough draft of the story. Then, because great care is needed, the rough draft is submitted to the department manager for a double check.

After the feature has been initialed by the department manager, any suggested changes are incorporated, and a neat copy is typed for submission to the editor's boss.

If the editor's boss approves the feature, it will bear the boss's initials and possibly changes. If there are changes, these are incorporated, and the material again is typed neatly and submitted to the next person for clearance. Because there is a considerable lapse of time involved in getting the clearances, virtually all stories should be written in feature style. It is almost impossible in a company publication to have timely material; so, for example, the editor should avoid the typical newspaper lead which would say, "Chairman John J. Jones announced today. . . ."

Just like a city newspaper, the company publication should have beats, which are cultivated for items. One caution to the editor is to come out of the ivory tower and get to know the production employees, janitors, and clerks, as well as the top executives.

Among the regular beats which the editor should cultivate is the office of the chairman or president. It is a good idea to get on good terms with the head person's secretary. This individual schedules the president's appointments, reads all the correspondence, and knows what is going on.

The purchasing agent knows who is buying what; the comptroller or treasurer authorizes all spending and can supply information on projects even before they are approved; and the personnel office or offices maintain records of employees and can keep the editor informed on significant changes in employee numbers and service anniversaries.

Research and development can tell about new products; safety can help prepare safety stories; the production manager has production records and can predict production milestones; the insurance department can give statistics about employee benefits; and the data processing department can tell who buys bonds, gives to United Campaign, etc.

Of course, the list will vary, company by company, and it is up to the editor to learn his organization thoroughly to develop significant stories for the publication.

The sources of stories would depend upon the audience to be served. An employee publication would try to build esprit de corps among the employees. A sales publication, on the other hand, would cater directly to the needs of the salesmen--tips to help the salesmen in their jobs, stories about top salesmen and how they perform, information about new products, sales promotions, contests, etc.

Above all, the editor should remember that the job is one of selling--selling ideas rather than products. Before the editor can sell something, he first must be sold on himself, then on the company and all it represents. He should be prepared to sell himself and his ideas to others, again and again and again and again. Like the church on the hill, he should keep ringing the bell to declare the glad tidings. The job never stops. It is not a job for the lukewarm, fainthearted, or easily discouraged. It is a job for a tough-minded, dedicated, sophisticated professional.

Chapter

10

SETTING GUIDELINES

A house journal without a goal is like a tramp steamer which has no set schedule. Therefore, before the company decides to publish, top management should set some very specific objectives.

These objectives should be written down and used as a blueprint to which the editor can refer, from time to time, to make sure the ship is on course. In this way, not only the editor, but also management, has a map to show where the publication hopes to be headed and whether it is headed in that direction. As pointed out earlier, without such a set of objectives, management probably is not sure what it wants the publication to accomplish. In this case, the publication is in a very precarious position in times of financial crises.

The objectives should be detailed enough so the editor and management can make periodic studies to see if the publication is conforming to the standard. Such checks can be done by a simple analysis of the contents. A content analysis is carried out by assigning each story of an issue to a category. In this way it can be noted if all of the desired categories have been covered in a given issue or over a period of several issues. A good guide for content analysis of company publications is discussed in <u>Effective</u> <u>Public</u> <u>Relations</u>, Cutlip and Center, fourth edition, starting on page 285.

The editor can meet his objectives most easily if he resorts to planning. This means an editor of any ability is not going to wait for things to happen or for news to walk in the door. He has to help things happen and work very hard to get stories which fit the categories needed to meet the objectives. To accomplish this, the editor should make up lists of proposed stories for several issues ahead.

For example, say that one category of story needed to meet the objectives is employee benefits. The editor should schedule a benefits story for the publication which will appear three or four months in the future. Similarly, if waste reduction or safety are categories, stories should be scheduled in these categories far enough into the future so the editor has time either to assign the story to an assistant or do his own interviewing, picture-taking, writing, clearing, and rewriting. It should be remembered that there is a fairly long lead time for most company publication stories and pictures.

The objectives of a publication will be designed to fill the needs of the company it serves. Although all organizations face at least some common problems, each company invariably has a few problem areas which are unique. This is why a publication must have its own set of objectives and cannot merely adopt a list of objectives used by another.

By the same token, the organization's problems and goals will change to meet changing times and conditions. This is the reason it is necessary to review objectives from time to time and make needed revisions. Management knows it cannot operate its company using 1930 guidelines. It follows, then, that management will realize the same principle applies to its publication.

Below is a copy of the statement of purpose which was used several years ago by The Firestone Tire & Rubber Company:

STATEMENT OF PURPOSE

To provide information to employees about company progress and products; to encourage good relationships by promoting company-sponsored recreation and other events; to promote safety, suggestions, loyalty to company and community activities; to encourage good citizenship; to give some economic education to employees and to create a "family" atmosphere among them; to create awareness of employee responsibility in making good products and helping in selling these products wherever possible, regardless of the type of job held; and to further youth activities of the company.

(Reproduced by courtesy of The Firestone Tire & Rubber Company)

It should be noted that the Firestone statement of purpose is generalized, rather than being spelled out in specifics. This was the choice of company management, which felt it best to be less rigid and leave more leeway to the editors.

If company management feels there is need to be more specific, then it should be more specific. A company might even go so far as to spell out 10 percent of each issue for economic education, 15 percent for safety, 10 percent for suggestions, etc.

It is the author's thinking that it is best if editors retain more flexibility, then spot check to make sure that specific stories are carried at stated intervals in the desired categories.

The decision is, of course, up to the company which is doing the publishing.

The overriding criterion is, "How should we establish the objectives so we can do the best job of communicating the company story to the specific audience?"

In meeting objectives and maintaining a well-edited publication, even the best editor will face serious problems in addition to budgets and staff.

One problem will be lack of time to do the job best; another will be constant pressure for editor and/or staff to take on additional duties. Still another will be pressure to lower the standards to save time and money.

The time element can be solved to an extent by planning ahead. Most persons go through a lot of waste motion and could improve efficiency if they would make a critical study of what they do and then figure out ways to cut out some of the wastage.

One important way time is wasted is in interviewing, especially in the unplanned interview.

Prior to the interview, the editor should decide exactly what facts are desired and then write down the questions to be asked. He should allot himself a specific length of time for the interview. After all questions have been answered, he should allow a brief time for small talk on subjects not necessarily germane to the in-

terview. The editor should keep in mind that the person being interviewed has a desk full of work to do, as does he, so he should
avoid being trapped into an hour-long discussion of football scores,
horse racing, golf games, or beauty contests. Some editors could
write enough copy for an eight-page monthly publication in the time
wasted in unproductive chatting.

The editor can similarly look at other aspects of the job and
find ways to eliminate wasted time. If, after a searching examina-
tion of the work schedule, the editor (and staff) finds the publication still is pressed for time, there should be a frank talk with
management concerning the situation. Maybe the workload is simply
too great to be handled by the available staff. If management is
unwilling to add enough staff to do the necessary work, some provision should be made to trim the workload to manageable proportions.

An adjunct to shortage of time is the problem of auxiliary
duties. The constant adding of other jobs, some related to the publication, some not, comes about in several ways. One of these is
ignorance by management of the amount of time needed to produce the
publication. One reason is that some executives may not appreciate
the difficulty of producing creative, persuasive copy, and the amount
of time needed to write such copy. Probably some company officials
will always think the editor has a sinecure. This means they will
always put pressure on him by assigning him more duties.

Additional assignments might take the form of the editor's being asked to take his own photographs, or of the staff's being asked

to take pictures for use other than for the publication. The editor might be asked to handle plant tours, prepare advertisements, frame pictures, run a projector, give talks, take charge of fund-raising drives, etc. Such auxiliary duties are fine, as long as they do not interfere with the publication and if they lead to a promotion.

The working situation for a company's publication staff will vary by organization. Some companies are strict and tight-fisted; some are benevolent. Some staffs are small and hard-pressed; some are large and relaxed.

The editor himself will provide some of the pressure for the addition of duties because he may be after a raise or promotion. Management may say or imply that the editor can expect advancement in pay or rank through proving himself more valuable. The editor then will try to prove his increased value by taking on the additional duties. This will be fine if some of the former duties can be delegated to other persons, or if the editor/staff really has become so proficient that additional jobs can be done without interfering with the primary job of producing the publication.

The danger is that the editor/staff really is working beyond capacity, so that some of the publication duties are sloughed off by the use of inferior or canned material.

There may also be pressure for the use of inferior material. Especially with the employee publication, there will be a steady stream of out-of-focus, poorly lighted snapshots of big fish, pet raccoons, vacation cottages, canoes, white mice, litters of dogs or kittens, an employee on water skis with the subject 1,000 yards away, etc. Occasionally, someone will submit a photograph which is in focus, is properly balanced, tells a story, and fits into the publication theme. Such photographs should be encouraged.

The publication policy should be specific in that all photographs used have to fit into the goals of the publication. Further, management should give the staff full authority to accept or reject any and all material submitted.

A good disposition of shutterbug snapshots would be their display for a few days on a specific bulletin board. The same applies for poems, letters from grandchildren, grade school themes, and other such items, unless such do serve the publication goals.

The overriding consideration for all material, whether staff-prepared or -submitted, is: Does this material fit in with the objectives of the publication? If so, is the material of sufficient quality so that it lives up to our standards?

No publication guideline or goal is complete unless it spells out how the goals are to be accomplished or implemented.

One aspect of implementation is a system of clearances, and a system of feedback--not only from the audience, but also from management.

If management fully understands what a publication can and cannot accomplish, the work of the editor will be infinitely easier. Also if management has a hand in the production from generation of ideas through distribution, management's thinking is constantly favorably inclined toward the project.

The only way management can be exposed constantly to the publication is by the editor himself. The editor cannot be shy, thin-skinned, or an ivory-tower dreamer. He must have constant contact with management, asking for ideas and suggestions. Of course, he should point out that not every suggestion can be used.

One very good method of constant exposure to management think-ing, and for inclusion of management in the publication, is the formation of an editorial board. If there is such a board it should include several persons of top and middle management representing the different facets of the company. The group should meet at spe-cifically stated intervals, probably monthly. The meetings should produce ideas for future issues of the publication(s) and critiques of the most recent issue.

The editor should run each meeting and make sure the meetings don't degenerate either into a defense of what he is doing, or into "Well done, George" sessions. The editor should seek straightfor-ward, honest criticisms and ideas for improvement.

To a great extent, the editor is the publication. Therefore, the success of the publication depends upon the editor. An editor is not going to take a three-week vacation trip without first es-tablishing some plans. By the same token, an editor cannot expect to have a successful publication without doing a lot of prior plan-ning.

Chapter

11

THE PUBLICATION'S CORPORATE NICHE

Part and parcel of implementing the publication's objectives is establishing the editor at a suitable spot in the corporate hierarchy.

If the editor is placed far down the chain of command, it will be difficult for him to reach the ear of management on questions which are vital. The editor is hired because the corporation is having trouble communicating. Therefore, it makes sense that the communicator should be placed close to top management, since he is supposed to communicate the thoughts of management.

If management messages have to be filtered through a long chain of command, there is no chance communication can be achieved from management to editor to audience.

It is important the editor have at least lower- or middle-management status to have the prestige necessary to command respect of those corporate types who respect nothing else but titles. If the editor is placed at the clerk level, there are sure to be some persons up the ladder, afflicted with the time-clock syndrome, who are going to insist the editor function as a clerk--be at the desk promptly at starting time, no straying from the desk during working hours, no idle talking with other employees during working hours, etc.

Persons afflicted with the time-clock syndrome never take into account those times when the editor works far into the night on a layout, or spends an hour at midnight interviewing employees on the night shift, etc.

The same types may try to keep the editor from going to meetings or conferences. These types will imply that the editor is trying to "have an extra vacation at company expense." Such individuals may remark that "you should have learned all there is to know while you were in college."

The further the editor is removed from the top official, the better the chance that someone up the line is going to garble the message, sometimes intentionally.

Probably the most crucial point is to have the publication placed in an area in which the personnel is familiar with publications and their problems. This is so because the flavor and emphasis of the publication is going to be slanted by the surroundings.

Perhaps the best location is in public relations, because public relations persons are used to handling communications. They have been trained to communicate.

If the publication is located in personnel, the editor may have to work in a "hostile" climate. Personnel employees sometimes have no training or tradition of effective communicating. Personnel often use the "take it or leave it" attitude in communications. Record keeping, in personnel, supersedes almost everything. The establishing of blame comes on strong in many of the attempts to communicate. A sample: "You have been a bad boy for these reasons. Please sign this reprimand, which will go into your permanent file. If you do this again, we will institute termination procedures against you."

Personnel probably would not think the publication particularly important; "So what if the deadline is Thursday, we want you to handle these other, more important, chores first."

It is bad from the standpoint of communicating to have the publication established in industrial or labor relations. Industrial or labor relations persons often have an attitude of "Tell them nothing. What they don't know won't hurt us." Or, "Why should we help the union by broadcasting the company position in the publication?"

Labor or industrial relations persons spend considerable time in negotiations, in which the contract is being hammered out in legalistic language with the aid of lawyers on both sides. Such persons tend to phrase their communications in a pseudo-legal language designed to hide or obscure the true meaning.

The result is that the editor might be constantly frustrated in trying to communicate in clear, precise language, while the industrial relations person might insist on obscuring the message with legalistic phrases designed to confuse rather than enlighten.

To a great extent, the organization is going to judge the importance of the publication by the position the editor holds in the corporate hierarchy. Thus, if the editor is a clerk, or just slightly higher in the chain of command, the rest of the organization is not going to take the publication seriously. Low status in the corporate structure is not going to prove fatal for a good editor, but such a situation can make the job harder and more frustrating. It is quite likely that editors who are placed in lowly positions in the organization are working for companies which have little or no idea why a publication is being produced. Usually, the organization which has made a thorough study of communications has well-defined goals and objectives for the publication, and the editor is situated fairly high in the organization.

By high placement in the organization, the editor reports directly to someone in a decision-making position. This means the editor has a short chain of command--a direct pipeline to top management. This results in a much better chance of management messages getting through to employees.

Chapter

12

CHOOSING THE FORMAT

If an organization is going to use written communications other than pamphlets, brochures, or letters, an early decision must be made whether the publication is to be a newspaper or magazine.

There is no consensus by editors or companies which is the best. Some use newspapers successfully, while others use magazines just as well.

Management should study the pros and cons before making a decision. On the basis of the findings, the company probably will discover that choosing the format is like anything else in life--there will have to be a compromise. This means a newspaper will have its strong and its weak points; a magazine will have its strong and weak points.

Either format can do a good job; either can turn out a total flop. The important thing is to have a knowledgeable editor and a knowedgeable management.

Both formats use the same basics--words and illustrations produced in ink on paper. More important than the format is well-

written, well-displayed content. If content is good, the reader
will not clearly prefer one format to another.

Readers, being creatures of habit, prefer what they are used
to. If the organization has long had a newspaper, the readers probably will think a newspaper is the better format. If the organization has had a magazine for a long time, there probably will be just
as fierce loyalty to that format.

The magazine is the most frequently used format for a company
publication, according to Operation Tape Measure of the International Association of Business Communicators, formerly the International
Council of Industrial Editors.

However, newspapers are in a strong second place. Undoubtedly,
newspaper editors and readers feel that a newspaper is better.
There have been some recent shifts from magazine to newspaper by
some managements, as well as shifts from newspaper to magazine. In
each case, the management undoubtedly felt the shift made for an
improved communications package.

Managements and editors may prefer a magazine, if pleasing appearance is more important than frequency of contact. Magazine
makeup usually is more imaginative because an art director generally has charge of the layout. The management that prefers a magazine will feel that packaging is more important than content, and
that a good appearance will help to enhance the company image.

This feeling is valid whether the magazine is picture- or
text-oriented. Few can argue that the former Life and Look and
the current Time, Playboy, and Reader's Digest present more excit-

ing exteriors than do the comparatively stodgy <u>New York Times</u>,
<u>Wall Street Journal</u>, <u>Kansas City Star</u>, etc.

Not only is a magazine more attractive, potentially, but the
attention can be focused more sharply, item by item, because the
magazine page is smaller. This means that, usually, features are
read item by item. Generally, there is no choice of items on a
page or two facing pages. This eliminates some of the distractions
injected by the larger newspaper page, where a dozen or more elements are all vying for attention.

Because magazines are smaller and compactly bound, they are
easy to store on a bookshelf or in a magazine rack. This means
magazines lend themselves as collector's items, for boxing and
storing in attics or on reference shelves. They do not deteriorate
easily and can be referred to years after the date of issue.

Magazines usually are printed on glossy paper. This not only
lends to their attractiveness, but also makes for better reproduc-
tion of art and text. Color printing in magazines almost always
comes off better than it does in newspapers.

Magazines also are thought of as being made for leisure reading. When a person sits down to read a magazine, he fully intends
to spend a considerable length of time. Because magazines are for
leisure, the writing is usually in a livelier feature style as opposed to the somewhat more rigid, inverted-pyramid newspaper style.

Along with these strengths, there are weaknesses.

The magazine, page for page, is more expensive to produce. It
probably costs double the newspaper cost because printing proce-

dures are more complicated. In addition, the more attractive slick paper is much more expensive than newsprint.

Binding the pages together in book or magazine injects another step into the production process and boosts costs.

The editorial and mechanical production of a magazine is more sophisticated and time-consuming. This means the editor has to be more experienced in layout and makeup to produce a magazine than a newspaper. This usually requires the services of an artist to help the editor in designing each issue. It also means there has to be much closer liaison with staff, printer, and photographer. It demands tighter writing to make the story fit the space.

Because the reader expects the magazine to be written in a sprightly feature style, it means the staff should be skilled at writing. If the writing fails to hold the reader's interest, he might discard the magazine and turn to something else. The same reader, on becoming bored with an item on a newspaper front page, merely skips to another item.

Because of the higher costs and greater time needed to produce them, magazines usually are issued less frequently than newspapers. Consequently, for the money, the organization is not in touch with its audience quite so effectively with a magazine. This also means the material is less timely and, therefore, a less effective com-munications packet from management to audience. The magazine is probably best as a long-range tool, with the editor working several months ahead.

Most newspapers used as organizational communications are tab-

loid, or half-sheet size. There are many advantages in using a
newspaper for a company publication, especially if it is an employee
publication and there is a desire for frequent communication.

The mechanical production costs of a newspaper are lower than
those of a magazine. The newspaper usually has much cheaper paper.
There is no bindery charge. Newspaper layout is less sophisticated,
so relatively inexperienced editors can do the makeup. There is
little or no need for a highly paid art director to do the layout,
although some newspapers in industry have art directors.

Because of lowered costs and shorter production time, the newspaper can appear more frequently, twice a month or weekly, as opposed to monthly or quarterly for a magazine.

The organization should decide, on the basis of needs, which
format to use. If speed, economy, and frequency are important, the
choice would be a newspaper. If prestige and appearance are the
major concerns, with cost and frequency of contact being less crucial, a magazine is the answer.

No matter which format, the editor's concern is to make maximum use of the resources at hand. The best way to maximize the
format is to use techniques which are used by successful publications.

To do this, the editor should get on the mailing lists of
publications which are prize winners in the annual contests sponsored by the International Association of Business Communicators.

A thorough study of these publications should be made to see
why they are prize winners; then the editor can adapt to his use

the techniques used by the best editors.

The next step is to send his publication to the IABC for evaluation. For a small fee, the IABC will critique the publication and make suggestions for its improvement.

Another step is to attend workshops and annual meetings of a local IABC chapter. A further step is to study top consumer publications, such as Better Homes and Gardens, Parade, Newsday, National Observer, and others. The editor should see what these publications do that is effective and adapt the techniques to his publication.

Planning is very important. Before the first issue of the publication is started, it should be planned for at least three issues in advance. Even newspapers should not be written from the "top of the head." Instead, a proposed list of stories should be prepared far ahead of the deadline, and management solicited for additional story suggestions. After story titles have been approved, the necessary interviewing and picture-taking should be done--again, far ahead of deadline.

A dummy should be prepared to indicate where stories and illustrations will go. The stories and pictures then can be scaled to the desired space, so that the layout is not thrown together at the last minute.

Whatever the format, the editor's guideline should be simplicity. The best guide in layout is to "help the reader to read." The editor should avoid layouts which are too arty, garish, gimmicky--round illustrations, slanting headlines, fancy overprints.

The most effective layout is one with stories and art tailored to the audience and laid out in a manner that will attract the eye.

It might be well to suggest a couple of good books as guides to attractive and effective layout for newspapers and magazines. They are: Publication Design by Roy Paul Nelson, William C. Brown Company, Publishers, and Ink on Paper by Edmund Arnold, Harper & Row, Publishers.

It should be kept in mind that the best current newspaper layout is horizontal. The following pages show examples of newspaper and magazine layout, plus examples of stories used in house journals.

Renewed hopes for newsmen missing in Asia

By Mark Mehler

Members of the U.S. Committee to Free Journalists held in Southeast Asia are "convinced" that at least some of the 19 missing newsmen in Asia are being held in Cambodian prison camps.

Peter Arnett, Associated Press special correspondent and a member of the committee, told E&P this week that the group had determined through interviews with former POW's from North Vietnam and U.S. diplomatic sources, that some of 19 missing newsmen—who include five Americans—are alive and being held by Cambodian insurgents (E&P April 28).

Last Friday, (November 2) Arnett; Walter Cronkite, chairman of the committee; and Richard Dudman of the St. Louis Post Dispatch, met for an hour with Secretary of State Henry Kissinger at the White House. The group told Kissinger of their firm belief that the newsmen were alive. Arnett said Kissinger agreed to bring up the matter in his discussion with Chinese Premier Chou En-Lai this week in Peking. Arnett said although Kissinger was not personally acquainted with the problem and "had to take our word for it," he nevertheless seemed "receptive."

The committee believes the insurgents, who have not had any direct communication with the U.S., are holding the newsmen in out-of-the-way prison camps as a possible bargaining lever in future talks with the West. Arnett said their plight was analogous to the POW's, locked away for five and six years in North Vietnam.

The committee is trying first to get a list from the Cambodians of all prisoners. Arnett said he didn't fear too much for their lives, since the newsmen were more valuable to the insurgents alive and no rational purpose would be served by killing them.

The group plans to meet with Kissinger on his return. They hope the Secretary can interest Chou En-Lai in intervening and using his considerable influence as a go-between in negotiations.

"We haven't pressed the issue to this point because we didn't want to confuse the civilian newsmen with the military issue of the POW's," explained Arnett.

Up to now, he added, the campaign has been deliberately low-key, buoyed by hopes that the newsmen would be released along with soldiers after the January ceasefire.

The group now plans to meet after Kissinger's return to plot a larger-scale publicity campaign, involving not only lobbying and pamphleteering, but possibly ads in major newspapers and electronic media.

The newsmen were captured by the North Vietnamese and later turned over to the Cambodian rebels, according to sources. Continued heavy fighting throughout Cambodia and the disorganized nature of the rebel forces in the earlier days of the fighting, have hindered the committee effort.

24

Guild strike fails to halt publication

The Newspaper Guild struck the Oakland Press, Pontiac, Mich. November 8, in the first major walkout in the paper's 130-year history.

Supervisory and other personnel have continued to publish, although most members of the craft and Teamsters unions have refused to cross guild picket lines.

Bruce McIntyre, vicepresident and editor of the Press, said the paper was two hours late last Thursday, less than an hour late on Friday, and has made its deadlines the last four days.

He said a "substantial" number of the 45 editorial workers represented by the guild have crossed the picket line and that engravers, supervisory composing room employes (in the ITU) and other supervisory personnel have put out the paper.

Non-union drivers have been picking up the paper for delivery at the loading dock in 20 rented vehicles. McIntyre said most of the trucks were being driven by "our own people." He said there has been some violence on the picket line and that two employes' cars have been vandalized outside the building.

"There are a bunch of picketers who are not guild or craft union people . . . I don't know who they are, but they're a rough bunch, and there have been some incidents of people getting punched around."

The issues, according to the guild, are a company demand for the right to demote employes and cut their pay scales and sick leave provisions.

McIntyre said the guild had been offered the same contract already ratified by the craft unions. He said the pay hike was a percentage increase and would therefore be even more for the guild than for the other unions.

Helen Fogel, administrative officer of Local 22 of the Newspaper Guild said the paper had not been meeting its deadlines and was putting out a "limited" paper.

She said management charges that the guild strikers have been stealing papers from deliverers were unfounded. She admitted she had heard of some newspaper carriers burning papers on their routes, but said "none have done this in my presence."

The two sides met November 12 and 13. Negotiations have been underway since May on a contract to replace the three-year pact which expired June 22.

•

Dixie Roto supplement resumes in New Orleans

Dixie Roto, the Sunday magazine of the New Orleans (La.) Times Picayune, will be back in print on Sunday, November 18, and will continue weekly publication thereafter. The printers of the roto magazine section missed only one issue, November 11. Ashton Phelps, publisher of the Times-Picayune, announced last month that the publication was being suspended due to the newsprint shortage (E&P, October 27).

PRESS ORDERED—Publisher Harry R. Horvitz (right) signs an order for a five-unit Harris N-1650 web offset press to print the Willoughby (O.) News-Herald, a 30,000-circulation p.m. daily. At left is James B. Roe, Harris sales representative. The press will be installed in a new building, now being constructed to house the press and reel-tension-pasters. The latter will be on a level below the press with web leads coming through slots in the pressroom floor. The new facility will be completed in the Spring of 1974. Horvitz also publishes the Lorain Journal, Mansfield News Journal, Dover Times Reporter, and the News Herald in Ohio, plus the Times Record of Troy, New York. Circulation of the five newspapers is 193,000 and aggregate employment is about 1,000.

White House reporters called 'stenographers'

Washington Post Pulitzer Prize-winning reporter Bob Woodward has attacked the White House press corps. Woodward, who shared the Pulitzer with Carl Bernstein for their Watergate exposes, called White House reporters "no more than sophisticated stenographers" with an "obscene affection for the official version of events."

He continued: "The Watergate has demonstrated that they were being lied to. And so these reporters have adopted what I would only characterize as a superficial toughness. They go to press conferences and think they're being great investigators by asking the President questions like, 'Don't you think you should resign?'" Woodward said.

Woodward spoke to members of the Liberal Party of the Yale Political Union in New Haven, Conn.

•

Walsmith resigns

W. A. Walsmith has resigned as general manager of NAPP Systems (USA) Inc., a joint venture of Lee Enterprises, Inc. and Nippon Paint Company, Ltd.

He will continue as vice president of NAPP Systems and as a consultant. Tom L. Williams, publisher of the Davenport (Iowa) Times-Democrat will serve as acting general manager until a new general manager is named.

EDITOR & PUBLISHER for November 17, 1973

Fig. 1—Example of vertical makeup. (Courtesy, Editor & Publisher)

Distribution center keeps 'em rollin'

It was early Sunday afternoon when the phone rang in the suburban St. Louis home. "Vandals slashed 60 school bus tires here overnight," the manager for Wells Stores in Washington, Mo., told Doug Woollard. "I need replacements right away so the buses can roll Monday morning."

Woollard, manager of distribution services, met the dealer at the St. Louis distribution center an hour later and provided the needed tires.

The buses ran on schedule.

Such off-hours crises are infrequent, but the facility handles four or five emergency orders every working day. Involving such things as adjustments and urgent needs of commercial trucking accounts, these orders go out the same day if they're in early enough—or within 24 hours.

Routine orders are shipped within 48 hours.

The function of the supporting warehouse is to provide fast service on auto, truck and farm tires and tubes in greatest demand.

Its customers are 42 Goodyear Service Stores and more than 200 dealers in an 80,000-square-mile area that includes parts of four states and a population of about 7.5 million.

Slower moving items are handled by the Topeka Distribution Center.

Triangle

75 YEARS OF LEADERSHIP

Vol. 55 — Monday, June 18, 1973 — No. 12

Nelson is the name. Rubber is his game. On Pages 4-5 you'll find a report on what a typical day in the tough metro New York market is like for this sales representative, one of more than 40 Chemical Division field men.

typical order

Processing each order involves many of the St. Louis facility's 17 office and 10 warehouse employes. Here's how a typical one is handled.

At 9 a.m. Tuesday morning the
(Continued on Page 2, Col. 1)

J. L. Mendler to be ARM-R at Chicago; 4 others advance

John L. (Lou) Mendler Jr., district manager at St. Louis, will be promoted to assistant region manager-retail for the Central Region at Chicago effective July 1, according to A. H. Shafer, vice president, Replacement Sales Division.

He will succeed Thomas H. Maxwell, who is being promoted to Goodyear International Corporation as sales director for Australia.

Shafer also announced the following related personnel shifts will take effect July 1:

Bill J. Pullen moves to St. Louis as district manager from that position at Omaha.

Dion R. (Dee) Welch, district manager-wholesale for New York Metro-NB, becomes district manager at Omaha.

N. D. (Dick) Hemric advances from assistant district manager-wholesale at Philadelphia to succeed Welch.

Mendler joined Goodyear in 1950 at Wilson, N.C., and served in budget sales in that state. He managed stores in the Carolinas from 1953 to 1956, then became ADM-R at Charlotte and Birmingham and ADM-W at St. Louis. Appointed DM at El Paso in 1960, he moved to that position at Des Moines
(Continued on Page 3, Col. 1)

| Mendler | Maxwell | Pullen | Welch | Hemric |

Doug Woollard checks progress as Joe Whitener, warehouseman at the St. Louis distribution center, pulls tires needed for an order by Harden Bros. Tire & Supply, Mt. Carmel, Ill.

Fig. 2—Example of front page of field sales publication. (Courtesy, The Goodyear Tire & Rubber Company)

Fossils discovered during parking lot test

Workmen, drilling in the parking lot in the early Spring, found fossils in the rock about halfway down each 25 foot hole that was drilled.

The fossils were embedded in sandstone and looked like scales and bones of fish.

"Actually, I'm not surprised," said one of the workmen. "All of the Barberton area was a swamp millions of years ago and this is where you'll find a lot of fossils," he said.

The men were hired according to county law to find out what type of soil will be supporting the new parking deck. Their findings determine the type of foundation that will be used and how deep the supports will be sunk into the ground.

Drillers, using a rotary rig, start drilling through the top few feet with an auger. They drill through the water table and switch to an industrial diamond bit when they hit stone. The drills are cooled with water to keep the bit from being worn away by friction. "In some areas of the country," said one of the men, "the rock is very hard and we burn through a bit every few feet. Each new bit costs $400."

In this area, the stone is a softer sandstone. The average depth of the holes drilled in the parking lot was 25 feet before substantial solid rock was hit. The drillers took samples of the core every five feet, labeled them and laid them on top of each other to show what the layers of the earth looked like under the parking lot.

While drilling into the parking lot in the Spring, workmen found fossils embedded in the rock samples.

MAGIC CAPSULE

Vol. IV, No. 6   The Barberton Citizens Hospital   June 29, 1973

The little daughter of Dr. and Mrs. G. I. Kim was busy watching everyone.

Dr. W. T. Wu and his wife Dr. Shwu-jen Su are both interns at BCH.

Doctors' families trade favorite food recipes

Delicious hot and cold dishes were prepared by the House Staff from recipes from their native countries for the International Smorgasbord on May 17.

There were foods from Taiwan, Egypt, Syria, Malaysia, India, Korea, Argentina, Mexico, Bolivia, and the United States.

Doctors and their wives and families were invited and over 100 people attended the banquet.

After dinner, Dr. M. S. Harvey, senior minister at First Methodist Church in Akron, surprised the interns and residents by giving a travelogue on his trips to a number of the doctors' native countries.

More than 100 people sampled dishes from around the world at the International Smorgasbord on May 17.

Fig. 3--Example of hospital publication, using horizontal make-up. (Courtesy, The Barberton Citizens Hospital)

At Raleigh —

"Recently we had an emergency order at a company in Hamilton, Ohio for shipment to our customer in Raleigh. Since this was my order going to one of my accounts I was particularly interested in the way it was handled. Your people did an excellent job and I express my thanks." **(Editor's Note: This letter was sent to Harold Brinkley, city dispatcher, and an employee since March 1955.)**

At Ft. Wayne —

"I want you to know I appreciate all the searching you've done for my company and one of our accounts. It's trucking companies like Roadway and people working for them like you that make doing business a pleasure." **(Editor's Note: This letter thanks Grace Favory, cashier, and an employee since December 1969.)**

At Pottsville, Pa. —

"Thank you for your most valuable and necessary assistance in obtaining the requested information on one of our consignments. It's indeed a great relief to know there remain some scattered outposts of service and efficiency available to us." **(Editor's Note: This letter was sent from a local hospital to T.L. McGarry, dispatcher/dock foreman on his handling of tracing of medicine from Houston, Texas to Pottsville. He has been an employee since April 1967.)**

At Dalton, Ga. —

"I'd like to thank you for the prompt service on our recent shipment to Grand Rapids. Roadway's work was exceptional. Our shipment did arrive in Grand Rapids on Monday as promised, and our customer was delighted. Needless to say, any business I can send your way in the future I will. I feel that any truck line that can pick up in Dalton on Saturday afternoon and deliver in Grand Rapids on Monday is certainly 'on the ball' and deserves the business."

At St. Louis —

"Recently your Charles Butler delivered a load of steel expansion tanks to our dock. He had a very helpful and cooperative attitude and assisted in every way to help us unload this equipment with complete efficiency. The clerical employees of our company were very complimentary of his manner. As an employer and businessman, I want you and your company to know that you should be proud to have a man such as him working for you. He is probably the best sales representative you have in your organization. Because of his attitude and cooperation I'm instructing our people in our factory in West Warwich, R.I. to make all our shipments to St. Louis via Roadway." **(Editor's Note: City Driver Butler has been an employee since 1952.)**

At Burlington, Iowa —

"Our family was involved in an accident which totaled our car and put my husband in the hospital and injured a friend who was riding with us. My husband and I both feel that if Raymond Long hadn't been there along with the other truck drivers to administer emergency first aid, my husband may have bled to death or had complications. He helped us in every way humanly possible. You are fortunate to have a man of this caliber working for your company. I feel safer knowing Roadway trucks are on our highways." **(Editor's Note: Long has been with Roadway since the terminal was opened here last June.)**

At Omaha —

"I want to extend my thanks for some of the finest service I've seen in the freight industry. I contacted Jim Carlin and Bill Murphy in your Omaha terminal and asked them if they could pick up a truckload in Dayton, Ohio on Thursday and deliver it here Friday. They made a few phone calls to Dayton and said they could. We had some problems with the shipper and Roadway didn't pull away from the dock until 2 a.m. Friday. They had this load on our dock at 9 p.m. the same day. This performance saved myself and our company a considerable amount of grief. Roadway will be remembered by me for many years to come." **(Editor's Note: Carlin is terminal manager here, and Murphy, sales representative.)**

At Cincinnati —

"We want to commend your company on the excellent job of expediting a shipment to us from Charlotte. We contacted your Charlotte operation Wednesday and told them of a rush shipment. We then contacted Garnett in your Cincinnati Tracing dept. and requested she keep us posted on the shipment. Thanks to her efficient handling the shipment was delivered Friday morning. We feel this is excellent service and wanted to let you know we appreciate the cooperation of your employees." **(Editor's Note: Tracing Clerk Garnett Howard has been an employee since March 1971.)**

(Editor's Note: Due to the numerous letters received in the last few months we're going to summarize some of the more lenghty ones. Sincere thanks has been sent for the work of Walter Curtis, terminal manager at Holland, Mich.; R.R. McGinnis, terminal manager at Meridian, Miss.; Road Driver Ralph Hacker of Cincinnati; P&D Driver Frank Pitrola of Buffalo; Road Driver Reese Davis of Meridian; General Office Clerk Charlotte Parker of Columbus, Ohio, and Tracing Clerk Debra Ruggeri of Laurel, Md.)

Fig. 4--Example of employee recognition through customer letters. (Courtesy, Roadway Express, Inc.)

GOOD YEAR
75
75 YEARS OF LEADERSHIP

the **wingfoot clan**

Akron Edition

The Goodyear Tire & Rubber Company

Vol. 62   Akron, Ohio, July 19, 1973   No. 29

Ceremonies start at 1 p.m. for historic run

Wingfoot Express rolls today

The Wingfoot Express line that launched the first interstate truck travel 56 years ago will roll again, starting with colorful ceremonies set for 1 p.m. today in front of the main lobby of corporate headquarters.

Employes who can be spared from their jobs are urged to attend the brief celebration and watch the departure of a 1915 Packard truck for Boston.

The event will feature the Goodyear band, an escort of antique cars and special presentations.

Highlighting Goodyear's 75th anniversary, the 12-day journey will recreate the Express in the days when it was the nation's pioneering long-distance truck line. The success of the Express convinced a doubting nation of the merits of pneumatic tires.

The company withdrew from the trucking business after proving the feasibility of its idea and went on to become the world's largest tire and rubber company.

Cruising at 17 miles an hour, the four-cylinder Packard will follow the old Lincoln Highway (U.S. 30) and Boston Post Road (U.S. 1) route of the original Wingfoot Express, which reached Boston in 19 days after a series of breakdowns, punctured tires, collapsed bridges and other mishaps.

Only slightly modified to reproduce as faithfully as possible the features of the 1917 Express, the two-and-one-half-ton Packard truck is driven by its owner, David T. Myers, 62, and his son, Peter, 31, both of Holt, Mich.

It will visit a score of towns and cities along its 750-mile route with stopovers of a day or more scheduled for Pittsburgh, Philadelphia, New York and Boston.

In most cities, the truck will be ceremoniously welcomed by civic officials, bands and escorts of antique vehicles owned and driven by local residents.

It was in 1916 that Goodyear announced that it would produce the first pneumatic truck tires and create a truck line to demonstrate their practicability.

At the time, most of the nation's nearly 1 million trucks were confined to intra-urban travel, limited by the solid rubber tires which minimized speed, provided poor gasoline mileage, often became mired in mud and delivered jolting, teeth-shattering rides.

Goodyear established the Wingfoot Express as an experimental truck line to carry finished rubber products to Boston and then go to Killingly, Conn., to pick up a load of cotton fabric used in those days to reinforce tires.

From the Killingly cotton mills, the trucks would return directly to Akron, a

(Continued on Page 3, Col. 1)

A CHURCH OF COMPARATIVE age in Hudson formed an appropriate background as the Wingfoot Express rolled along on a recent practice run. The 1915 Packard leaves today for Boston in an effort to recreate the 1917 Akron-to-Boston run that helped convince the nation interstate trucking was feasible. See more on the Express on Page 3.

MORE THAN HALF A CENTURY of development and improvement separates the 1915 Packard that is serving as the 1973 Wingfoot Express and the monster that rolls across today's highways. David Glemming, tire test division, had to look up at the modern truck as he stood on the 17½-foot-long Packard's running board.

MIP progress for 6 months

This is the latest report covering six months' operation of the Monthly Investment Plan through which employes may purchase Goodyear common shares. The plan is entirely voluntary and Goodyear pays all brokerage commissions. Information on the plan may be obtained from the Cashier's Department (phone 7170) or any office of Merrill Lynch, Pierce, Fenner & Smith, Inc.

	Purchase Price	Number Shares	Number Participants
January, 1973	30.377	6,455	4,711
February, 1973	28.010	6,948	4,732
March, 1973	29.042	6,839	4,742
April, 1973	26.588	7,230	4,706
May, 1973	27.263	6,951	4,657
June, 1973	25.497	7,303	4,620

Since the start of the plan in September 1967, and after adjusting for the two-for-one stock split on April 15, 1969, a total of 397,040 shares have been purchased by employes at an average cost of $28.88 per share.

Company expands tuition aid program for employes

Liberalization of Goodyear's Educational Assistance Program for employes is announced, effective with all courses that begin after Sept. 1.

Two major improvements are provided in the revised undergraduate program. These are:

1) No prior college education is required. Previously an employe must have completed at least two years of college to be eligible.

2) Participants in the program will be reimbursed for 100 per cent of their tuition upon completion of each approved subject. Previously, 50 per cent of the tuition was reimbursed upon completion of a subject and the remaining 50 per cent was reimbursed upon graduation. (Employes already enrolled in the program and who had 50 per cent of their tuition withheld will not be reimbursed until they graduate.)

Any full-time employe who is on the active payroll at the time of application is eligible to receive reimbursement. Reimbursement is made only when tuition assistance is not received from any other source, including veterans' benefits.

Also, reimbursement is for tuition only and does not include books, general fees, laboratory fees, parking and other items. All classwork must be taken on the employe's own time. There is no restriction as to the number of credit hours per year per participant.

Under the revised program special emphasis will be aimed at course work that relates directly to the company's needs and the employe's present or future employment with the company. Courses of study not normally used in the company are not eligible for tuition assistance. Examples are education, music, physical education, pre-law, pre-medicine, and social work.

Courses must be taken for credit and a satisfactory grade received. Non-credit courses that are audited are not eligible for reimbursement. To be eligible for reimbursement, courses must be approved by the employe's department manager. Reimbursements under this program are, by law, treated as income and normal taxes are withheld.

Reimbursement also applies to graduate studies. Any full-time employe who has a bachelor's degree from an accredited college may participate in the graduate study program. This program pays the entire cost of tuition only, upon satisfactory completion of each approved subject taken in the normal quarter or semester pattern.

Approval for reimbursement for law degrees will be based on the necessity for this training in conjunction with the employe's present job or possible future job.

(Continued on Page 2, Col. 1)

Fig. 5--Example of page one layout and use of down-style flag. (Courtesy, The Goodyear Tire & Rubber Company)

Season's
Greetings

Fig. 6--Example of two front pages, using flag on page two.
Example continues on next page. (Courtesy, The Firestone Tire &
Rubber Company)

Firestone NON-SKID

**Published by and for employees of
The Firestone Tire & Rubber Company**

Vol. 58   December 20, 1973   No. 42

'My Most Memorable Christmas'
Employees Recall Past Holidays

NOTE: Christmas is made of memories. The warmth and emotion of bygone Christmas celebrations live only in the mind. But, like fine art and good wine, they can be brought out from time to time to be savored and enjoyed. Following are three stories written by Firestone employees who agreed to share their most memorable Christmases with our readers.

1951

"CHRISTMAS of 1951 stands out in my mind as most memorable," says Lee Alderdice, employee training supervisor at the Los Angeles plant. A retired Air Force Major, Alderdice is one of many servicemen who spent Christmas away from home, "but 1951 was worse than usual.

"I had expected to spend Christmas with my wife and three children in California when I received those dreaded orders. I left for England with the Strategic Air Command Christmas Eve day, but because of aircraft trouble, we were forced to land in Bermuda.

"When we departed, it was midnight Christmas Eve. Feeling very lonesome, and a little sorry for myself, I picked up the intercom to wish the crew 'Merry Christmas.' Somehow this didn't seem to be enough, so after a few choked up moments and a short prayer, we sang Christmas carols.

"This was an unforgettable Christmas for me as the remainder of the flight didn't seem as long and everything appeared just a little brighter. I thank God tears don't effect radio equipment as we would have had 10 electrical fires that night."

1948

CAROLYN MULLINS, who works in the comptroller's office at Firestone's Nashville plant recalls Christmas, 1948:

"Snow covered the ground. It had already been a very cold year. For Middle Tennessee farmers, the year had not been a very prosperous one. Our family had

four children—ages 11, 10, 8, 7 (I was 10). Not having any money had not really bothered us until early November. Then we began thinking of Christmas. Of course we whispered among ourselves, 'reckon we'll get **anything** for Christmas?'

"This was discussed for more than a month and finally a major decision was reached. We decided that if we **pretended** we would have a nice Christmas—that we actually would.

"We decided to get a Christmas tree—the biggest and prettiest ever! We went into the woods and chopped down several, trying to select the best. We brought it to the house, and Mama got out the old decorations (that still have memories). Our only heat then was the fireplaces and the old wood stove in the kitchen.

"OF COURSE the tree was beautiful—just as we knew it would be. With the smell of the fireplace burning and the smell of cedar, we were all set for Christmas. Mama said a couple of times during the evening, 'You children know there isn't much money this year, don't you?' We said, 'Yes' And kept right on talking

(Continued on Page 3)

Our Cover

Firestone's Supervisor of Photography, Dick Cernik, captured the spirit of a childhood Christmas for the Non-Skid's 1973 Christmas cover. The giant Raggedy Ann doll is part of a 'Winter Wonderland' display at O'Neil's Department Store in Akron. Raggedy has her arm around four year old Barbara Jolly, daughter of Mr. and Mrs. Richard Jolly. Her father is a curing supervisor at Plant 1, Akron.

Fig. 6 (Continued)

104

Decision ERT-41
Grievance A-15267
Dept. 231-B, Plant 2 Industrial Products,
Compound Room
Umpire: Edwin R. Teple

Nature of the Case

Whether or not a piecework rate was properly adjusted.

Background

In April, 1968, the mill and banbury put-up operations were combined. The wage payment for the serviceman who serviced the put-up operators was based on a percentage of their earnings. Operation 35 was used to pay the serviceman on shifts when no mill batches were put-up, and Operation 82 was used on shifts when both the mill put-up and banbury put-up pools had to be serviced. Operation 82 was used until July 1, 1968. At this point a general wage increase took effect, and the company changed the percentage for Operation 82, which gave rise to this grievance.

Union Position

The union understood the retention of Operation 82 as calculated and accepted it when the agreement on the job combination was reached. If there was to be a change in the percentage used for this operation, it should have been made when the supplemental agreement was written.

Company Position

The earnings potential of the put-up pool was increased with the higher mill put-up rates, and the serviceman's rate is based on the put-up pool's earnings; therefore, it was proper to change the ser-viceman's rate to keep the same relationship between the pool and the service jobs.

Umpire Analysis

In the umpire's opinion, the reduction in the percentage for Operation 82, beyond the adjustment connected with the general wage increase, was a violation of the supplemental agreement of April 29, 1968. It is the umpire's decision that this grievance must be sustained.

Award

The employes in the serviceman classification are to be reimbursed for their loss in earnings as a result of the company's unilateral reduction in the percentage for Operation 82 on July 1, 1968.

Decision ERT-42
Grievance B-16352
Dept. 315-B, Metal Products
Umpire: Edwin R. Teple

Nature of the Case

Wheather or not a one week suspension of the grievant was for just cause.

Background

Shortly after 5 p.m. on March 16, 1970, employes on the second shift process lines in the company's Metal Products Plant started leaving their jobs as a result of a dispute arising out of the suspension of a welder operator. Some employes finished the shift on other jobs, but people who had gathered around the plant gate prevented the third shift from coming in.

Thirty-six of the process line employes who originally left the plant and initiated this work stoppage were suspended for one week for this violation of the no-strike clause. Ten others from the process lines, together with seven additional persons who were found actively engaged in picketing or preventing others from entering the plant, were given greater penalties. The grievant was in the latter group and eventually received a one-week suspension.

Union Position

The grievant did not participate in the walkout on March 16, and did not take part in any picketing. The union also denies that he stood in the gate or interfered with anyone trying to go to work.

Company Position

The company takes the position that the grievant, by his activities on the picket line in front of the plant gate, was deemed to be actively participating in the illegal action and therefore subject to discipline.

Umpire Analysis

As the umpire has indicated in the previous cases, attachment to a group engaged in picketing around a plant entrance, even for a limited time, may justify a penalty above and beyond smaller penalties imposed upon those taking part in the initial walkout. However, returning to the gate area only long enough to find out whether the people are returning to work, or passing the gate on the way to another destination, cannot be treated as taking part in the picketing.

Award

It is the umpire's award that the grievant be reimbursed for all time lost during the period of his suspension.

Page 4—The Wingfoot Clan—July 19, 1973

Fig. 7--Example of one way to report grievance meetings through an employee publication. (Courtesy, The Goodyear Tire & Rubber Company)

the **wingfoot clan**

Akron Edition | The Goodyear Tire & Rubber Company

**Published weekly in the interest of
employes of
The Goodyear Tire & Rubber Company
Akron, Ohio 44316
An Equal Opportunity Employer**

**Offices on Third Floor
Building Four
Inside Phone 4142
Outside, Dial 794-4142**

**Affiliated with the International Association
of Business Communicators, Akron Chapter.**

Editor . . . . Ed Ford
Associate Editor . . . . Rick Steinle
Staff Writer . . . . Fredrick Haymond
Staff Assistant . . . . Irene Poulos
Staff Artist . . . . Robert R. Wise

Vol. 62   Thursday, July 19, 1973   No. 29

Page 5

Fig. 8--Example of masthead. (Courtesy, The Goodyear Tire & Rubber Company)

Sales, earnings set new highs in 1973

The General Tire & Rubber Company recently reported record 1973 consolidated sales of $1,379,966,000 and net earnings of $76,846,000. T. F. O'Neil, Chairman, and M. G. O'Neil, President, announced at the Company's Board of Directors meeting in Washington, D. C., that these record earnings reflect a significant increase in operating earnings compared to 1972, primarily as a result of a strong first half.

The announcement pointed out, however, that the ratio of operating earnings to sales deteriorated in the second half of the year, and particularly so in the Tire and Plastics Divisions where the decline was substantial, reflecting increased raw material and labor costs which could not be passed through because of government price controls, prolonged strikes, and development and start-up costs of the Company's radial tire program.

The impact of these conditions has continued into 1974 and is now further compounded by the energy crisis, the economic slowdown, and particularly the decline in automotive production.

"Our outlook for 1974," President O'Neil said, "centers around the overall level of the economy, particularly as affected by the oil situation since so much of our business and that of our major customers depends on the solution of this unprecedented problem. Most areas of our business were affected in the latter months of 1973 by skyrocketing raw material costs and raw material shortages and they will continue to reflect the effects of the current situation in the months ahead.

Consolidated sales were 26.2% higher than 1972's volume of $1,093,477,000, the previous record high. All divisions of the Company contributed to the record sales.

The 1973 operating earnings were $77,512,000, or $3.65 per share. In 1972 they were $65,290,000, or $3.25 per share. The net earnings including extraordinary items were $76,846,000, or $3.62 per share based on 21,083,959 shares outstanding. This compares with 1972's restated net earnings of $74,839,000, or $3.73 per share computed on 19,876,034 shares then outstanding before the acquisition of the Aerojet-General minority interest in November, 1972.

All per-share figures have been adjusted to reflect a 2% stock dividend which the Board declared in addition to the regular quarterly cash dividend of 27.5¢ per share on Common Stock. The cash dividend is payable on February 28, 1974, and the stock dividend is payable on April 19, 1974, both to holders of record on February 4, 1974.

Also a factor in the earnings was the effect of the consolidating for the first time of the Company's equity in earnings of foreign subsidiaries and associated companies. This results in an 8¢ per share increase in 1973's operating earnings and a 5¢ per share increase in the restated 1972 figures.

Among the extraordinary items affecting the net 1973 earnings was a $2,035,000 after-tax provision taken by RKO General to reduce the book value of a CATV property, owned by its subsidiary, Cablecom General, to the estimated market value.

The earnings of both the Industrial Products and Plastics Divisions were new highs while the Tire Division's earnings were lower, reflecting the cost-price squeeze, increased expenses related to radial tires, and the impact of the longest strike in the Company's history. (The Mayfield, Ky., plant was idle 110 days during the year.)

Aerojet-General, now a wholly-owned subsidiary, achieved earnings of $17,945,000 on sales of $419,797,000, the highest earnings in Aerojet's 31-year history. The earnings include receipts from the sale of some of its

(Continued on page 2, col. 1)

Vol. XLIII Akron, Ohio, January 31, 1974 **No. 2**

Ken O'Brock; he wears many hats

If a man does not keep pace with his companions, perhaps it is because he hears a different drummer. Let him step to the music which he hears, however measured or far away.
Henry David Thoreau

The quote above best describes my thoughts as I listened to and got to know the man that is Ken O'Brock. There is a certain serenity about the man . . . a calmness and contentedness that comes through even though he leads a particularly busy life . . . a life where he must wear many hats and shoulder responsibilities that cannot be put off even for a day.

To most people at the Technical Center on Gilchrist Road, Ken is a competent and likeable lab technician, a 10-year veteran of General, with steel gray hair that belies his 34 years. But to other people Ken is the man who sold them a windmill, or the man who fixed it. Still more people know him as the city-boy turned dairy goat farmer, and a good one at that. And others know him in still another way . . . as a man who is very innovative—always in search of ways to do things better or faster or in a new way.

"I would have to describe myself as enthusiastic. Mostly over new or rediscovered methods of being self-sufficient. I recently lowered my oil

(Continued on page 2, col. 1)

Ken O'Brock

General-ly Speaking wins three awards

General-ly Speaking captured three awards at the recent International Association of Business Communicators (IABC) awards dinner for its efforts in United Fund - Red Cross coverage.

Charles Booth, Chairman for the 1973 Campaign, awarded the paper a first place trophy for "Page One Treatment," a third place plaque for "Year-round Coverage" and a third place plaque for "Campaign Coverage."

The yearly contest honors local in-house publications for their efforts in bringing the UF - Red Cross story to the community.

Fig. 9—Example of page one of General-ly Speaking, company publication of The General Tire & Rubber Company. (Courtesy, The General Tire & Rubber Company)

Main Street Receives Needed Attention

Main Street, just south of the Jackson Street Gate, will continue to be closed for approximately three more months. The street is closed so that it can be straightened between Jackson Street and the new Bartges Street.

For the next three months the following regulations will remain in force:

Employee drop-offs and pick-ups are being permitted on Main Street. However, no passenger vehicles are permitted south of Falor Street. U-turns are permitted at Falor Street so that cars can drop-off and pick-up passengers and return north on Main Street.

All employees are cautioned to use the cross-walks on the south side of Falor Street for their personal safety during this period.

The Metro Transportation Company (MTC) is maintaining bus transportation on Main Street. Employees wishing to catch a south-bound bus can do so at the designated stop in front of Bldg. 24 on the west side of Main Street. Employees wishing to catch a north-bound bus can do so at the designated stop in front of the World Headquarters Building on the east side of Main Street.

Also, the Erie Railroad currently is replacing the grade-crossing north of Goodrich Street. This work is being done in two phases — with one-half of Main Street being closed during each phase. Two-way traffic is still being maintained. This project should be completed by June 1, according to City officials.

Employees parking in the Gate 17 and Bldg. 41 Garage are still being permitted to park in their respective areas. All employees are cautioned to exercise extreme care in driving and crossing streets in this area.

The City of Akron is providing signs and patrolmen to minimize the current traffic confusion surrounding the Akron Complex.

B.F.Goodrich

The Akron Citizen

VOLUME 14 NO. 7   APRIL 13, 1973

Original Equipment

Detroit Buys More BFG Tires

BFG employees will be seeing more of their work in 1973 automobiles rolling out of Detroit. The major auto manufacturers are turning more and more to radial tires on new model cars.

This year General Motors has selected the Company's top-of-the-line radial tires as optional equipment for the Chevrolet Monte Carlo; the Buick Electra 225 and the Buick Riviera; the Pontiac Grand Am and Gran Prix; and all models of the Cadillac will feature BFG tires as optional equipment. No General Motors cars have radial tires as standard equipment on 1973 models.

The other big auto-maker, Ford Motor Company, has BFG radials as optional equipment on the Maverick and some full-size Fords and on the Mercury Comet. Radials are standard equipment on full-size Mercurys.

There has been a sharp increase in the number of BFG radials now used by the auto companies. In 1972, for example BFG radials were used as optional equipment on Cadillacs, Mavericks, Comets. BFG radials were standard equipment on Lincolns in 1972.

It is apparent that BFG's forecasting of the acceptance of the radial tire as original equipment is coming true. P. C. Ross, president, B.F.Goodrich Tire Company, has said that by 1976 "two out of three new cars will be equipped with radial tires."

He added that sales of radial passenger tires in the replacement market will grow at an average rate annually of 38 percent in the next few years thus making radials the fastest growing segment of the tire industry.

This was the scene a few weeks ago when work began on the straightening of Main Street just south of BFG's Jackson Street Gate.

Akron Improvement Program
Now Progressing In Five Areas

Work is now in progress in five different areas of the Akron Plant as part of the Facilities Improvement Program.

In Bldg. 9-A, Tire Treads, the lunchroom is being remodeled. A new ceiling, a new exhaust fan and repainting are included among the improvements. Also in Bldg. 9-A, new metal panel inserts are replacing the windows on the Main Street side of the room.

In Bldg. 36-A, endless Flat Belts, the locker room is receiving major attention. The room is being enlarged, and new fixtures, new flooring and new partitions are being installed.

In Bldg. 36-B, another endless Flat Belt area, the men's rest room is being repaired, relighted and repainted. A new wall is being added at one end to screen some insulated piping, and a new exhaust fan is being installed. The women's rest room in Bldg. 36-B is being repainted, and a new exhaust fan is being added.

Meanwhile, new electrical wiring and brighter lights are being installed in Bldg. 35-B, Cutless Bearings, and in Bldg. 220-D, Flat Conveyor Belts. Repainting will follow in these two areas.

The painting of Bldg. 35-C, Cutless Bearings, was recently completed.

License Plates
Still On Sale

The BFG Employees Store reports that the sale of 1973 license plates will be extended through Monday, April 16. The new plates must be on your car by midnight on Monday.

Employees may still buy their Ohio plates during the regular store hours of 7:30 a.m. until 5:15 p.m., today and Monday.

License plates for 1973 cost $10 plus a 50 cent fee. There is also a $5 permissive tax for those applicable counties.

Employees are asked to bring their registration card and automobile title with them when they purchase their plates. The BFG store reports that it is also important that employees know their taxing districts when they purchase plates this year.

BFG Begins Three
Anti-pollution Projects

Three anti-pollution projects costing nearly $1 million will soon be under way at BFG plants in Akron, Oaks, Pa. and Fort Wayne, Ind.

In Akron, a coal-fired boiler will be converted to oil fuel at a cost of approximately $450,000 in a step to meet provisions of the Federal Clean Air Act and Ohio air pollution regulations. The boiler will retain its ability to use coal if needed.

Although BFG's Akron boilers now use mechanical collectors to reduce particulates, the conversion will eliminate a high percentage of the sulphur dioxide emission. The conversion work will begin in May and will be completed this fall.

At the BFG tire plant in Oaks, a coal-fired boiler will be converted to oil and/or gas this summer at a cost of $275,000, reducing particulates and sulphur dioxide from the atmosphere.

At the Fort Wayne tire plant, a primary waste water treatment system is being built at a cost of $260,000. A dual-section retention basin of 790,000-gallon capacity will store plant waste water for 24 hours prior to discharge. The basins will reduce the suspended solid content of the water and prevent floatable materials from entering the nearby Maumee River. Belt skimmers will be provided to remove floatable materials, including oil, as they accumulate.

Fig. 10--Example of page one of The Akron Citizen, employee publication of The B. F. Goodrich Company. (Courtesy, The B. F. Goodrich Company)

If 10¢ profit per dollar is 'fair,' what's 4.7¢?

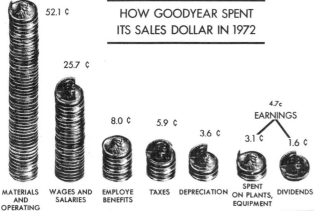

HOW GOODYEAR SPENT ITS SALES DOLLAR IN 1972

52.1 ¢ — MATERIALS AND OPERATING
25.7 ¢ — WAGES AND SALARIES
8.0 ¢ — EMPLOYE BENEFITS
5.9 ¢ — TAXES
3.6 ¢ — DEPRECIATION
3.1 ¢ — SPENT ON PLANTS, EQUIPMENT
1.6 ¢ — DIVIDENDS
4.7c EARNINGS

the wingfoot clan

GOOD\YEAR — 75 YEARS OF LEADERSHIP — Akron Edition

The Goodyear Tire & Rubber Company

Vol. 62   Akron, Ohio, March 15, 1973   No. 11

How much does Goodyear make on each dollar's worth of goods it sells?

Most Americans believe companies like Goodyear make 28 cents on each dollar of sales, according to a recent survey by Opinion Research Corporation.

Many of the people thought a profit of 28 cents was reasonable, but most felt 10 cents would be enough.

Goodyear would settle for 10 cents. It actually made less than half of that last year—4.7 cents profit on each sales dollar, the same percentage of profit the company made in 1963.

You'd think the world's largest rubber company could do better than that.

But making a 4.7 per cent profit from sales is fairly typical of all American business. And even that is quite a struggle.

Goodyear hasn't done better than 4.7 cents since 1969, and its profit was even lower in 1970 when a strike cut it to 4 cents.

Selling more goods doesn't necessarily mean earning more per sales dollar. Goodyear's total sales were higher in 1972 than in 1971, but its expenses and costs went up. So its profit margin remained at 4.7 cents per dollar, the same as the year before.

Even then, the profit doesn't gather dust in a vault. The company must spend millions of it every year to build new plants, modernize and expand older ones, and provide jobs.

That took 3.1 cents out of the 4.7 cents profit earned on each sales dollar.

But even that wasn't enough to pay for the $307 million Goodyear spent last year for more plants and equipment. The company had to borrow another $180 million.

The 1.6 cents remaining out of the origi- (Please turn to Page 3)

If 10¢ is 'fair,' what's 4.7¢?

(Continued from Page 1)
nal 4.7 cents profit per dollar was paid to Goodyear shareholders as a return on their investment.

That payment to shareholders, by the way, represented only 2.8 per cent of their investment, based on the closing price of Goodyear stock on Dec. 31, 1972. That's less than they could have earned by putting their money in a bank.

Starting with sales of $4,071,522,501 plus other income for a total of $4,095,912,318, here's how Goodyear spent its sales dollar in 1972:

MATERIALS & OPERATING—These costs of $2,134,985,287 took less of the sales dollar—52.1 cents—in 1972 (see chart) than the 52.5-cent share in 1971.

Materials include supplies, as well as raw materials used in Goodyear products, and operating expenses cover such items as freight, rent, utilities, advertising and interest on borrowed money.

WAGES & SALARIES—This portion, $1,052,200,268, was actual pay for time worked. It was the largest year-to-year increase of any category as a share of the sales dollar.

EMPLOYE BENEFITS—The total of $327,404,458 covers pensions, life insurance, hospitalization and Social Security, and includes pay amounting to $118,132,102 for vacations, holidays and other time not worked.

TAXES—Paid to federal, state, local and foreign governments in income and property taxes, excluding Social Security and excise taxes, this figure was $242,129,600.

DEPRECIATION—This amount, $146,033,942, represents the cost of replacing machinery and equipment as it wears out.

DIVIDENDS—The smallest part of the sales dollar, dividends totaling $63,940,726 were paid to Goodyear's shareholders out of profits.

RETAINED—This part, $129,218,037, is spent by the company on new and more efficient machinery and on modernizing and expanding plants and building new ones.

Fig. 11--Example of economic education story. (Courtesy, The Goodyear Tire & Rubber Company)

Two employes can verify benefits of wearing safety glasses at work

If either John Burket of the machine shop or Dana Hart of Research stops you and starts extolling the benefits of safety glasses, don't think they need a long rest in the country.

Both are still "coming down" after related accidents that would have left each of them with only one eye.

It's difficult to determine who was the more fortunate, but based on the details of the accidents, the nod might go to Dana Hart.

A research engineer in the exploratory section of polyester research and development, Hart was running a routine spinning operation for polyester yarn when his accident happened.

"I was bending over to turn one of the switches on the high speed spinning unit when one of the spools exploded right beside my face," Hart said. "The explosion threw me up against the wall."

Hart was hit by three jagged pieces of plastic shrapnel, one of which deflected off the frame of his gold-rimmed safety glasses and cut his forehead above the eye.

"It definitely would have put the eye out," Dana said. "We estimated that the piece was traveling at 120 miles per hour. When you're a foot away that doesn't give you a lot of time to get out of the way."

Hart was conscious throughout the accident and received immediate first aid from fellow researchers. He was on his way to the hospital in six minutes.

A shift foreman in the machine shop tool room, Burket also was involved in fairly routine work when his "instant accident" took place.

"I was standing beside one of my men who was prying a torque tap part for a numerical control machine. We were working with the part locked in a vise when a tiny piece broke loose under the stress.

"I heard a tick and suddenly couldn't see anything out of my left eye. I took the glasses off and saw the whole left lens

(Please turn to Page 3)

THE EYES HAVE IT as two employes piece together accidents that proved the merit of wearing safety glasses. John Burket (top), machine shop shift foreman, holds the tiny piece of metal that shattered the right lens of his spectacles. Dana Hart, Research, looks at the much larger plastic projectile that glanced off his glasses and left a gash in his forehead.

Safety glasses

(Continued from Page 1)

was shattered as if it had been hit with a hammer. I blinked a couple times to make sure my eyes were all right."

An Apprentice School graduate, Burket has been a shift foreman for six years and has 21 years of service.

The area where Burket's accident happened is one of the machinery division sections in Building 41 where safety eyeglasses are mandatory. Goodyear is in the process of providing safety glasses for all employes who work in Building 41 either permanently or temporarily like maintenance personnel. All machinists in the building now wear safety glasses.

Don Grayem, corporate safety, said the eye protection program for Building 41 is 90 percent complete and will be finished when all prescription glasses have been ordered and distributed.

Fig. 12--Example of safety story. (Courtesy, The Goodyear Tire & Rubber Company)

1971 absenteeism cost employes $2.8-million

How would you like to lose $2.8-million in one year?

That sum of money may sound like part of a Howard Hughes saga, but the loss of $2.8-million happened right here in Akron.

Hourly employes of the Akron plants lost nearly $2.8-million in earnings last year as a result of one thing — absenteeism.

"Last May we projected the 1971 figure would be more than $2.5-million, but the final results are somewhat higher than expected," said Jim Culler, personnel manager, Akron plants.

One of the most misunderstood topics in industry, absenteeism has far-reaching results that extend beyond the simple "you're not here, you don't get paid" formula.

"When absenteeism of skilled employes results in lower production or affects our quality, customer demands cannot be met," Culler said. "When production and quality decline, so do sales. Then jobs can also slip away."

Fortunately, the problem of absenteeism can be met and surmounted. The solution lies in realizing that excessive absenteeism, the kind that loses $2.8-million in wages for Goodyear families, slows productivity and makes Goodyear less effective in the market place.

"When that happens, employes' job security is undermined and the company's ability to compete is severely weakened," Culler said. "It's too early to estimate what the loss in earnings will be for this year, but we hope for a big reduction in absenteeism. Cutting absenteeism helps the entire Goodyear family."

Fig. 13--Example of absenteeism story. (Courtesy, The Goodyear Tire & Rubber Company)

what our competitors are doing

The U.S. Export-Import Bank has approved a direct loan of $13 million to Romania for construction of a tire plant. General Tire International is providing technology, engineering services and training for the plant that will have an annual capacity of one million radial tires.

* * *

Production of steel wire for tire cord is scheduled to begin in February, 1974 at Firestone's Danville, Ky., Wire & Cable Company, the firm announced. Firestone also operates a steel tire cord plant in Lens, France.

* * *

Gates Rubber has announced introduction of radial tires reinforced with Du-Pont's new Fiber B. Denver-based Gates said it is using the fiber in the belts for several sizes of a new line of luxury radial tires.

* * *

Michelin has announced opening of a regional headquarters with a warehouse and distribution center in Denver. It will serve dealers in Colorado, Utah and Wyoming. Michelin said it is one of four regional distribution points for off-the-road tires.

* * *

Cooper Tire reported it will begin regular production of radial tires this year at its Texarkana plant. It is the first part of a three-year, $7 million capital expenditure program. Cooper currently markets radial tires supplied by Kleber-Colombes, French tire maker.

Fig. 14--Example of competition story. (Courtesy, The Goodyear Tire & Rubber Company)

Recreation program judged finest in U.S. and Canada

For the second time in 10 years, Goodyear's recreational program in Akron has been judged the finest in the United States and Canada.

Chuck Bloedorn, recreation director, accepted the Helms Award Monday in Indianapolis at the annual National Industrial Recreation Association (NIRA) conference. Goodyear last won the award in 1962 for its Akron program and thus becomes the first company to be presented the honor twice for the same plant location.

NIRA annually presents the award to a company with the best overall recreational program.

Bloedorn credited "a fine staff and the more than 1,000 volunteers" for the success of the recreational programs.

In a report to the NIRA, he estimated 142,579 persons actively participated in regular Goodyear activities in 1972. That figure was up more than 3,000 from the previous year.

The director also pointed out more than 568,000 persons witnessed the variety of recreational displays and shows. The sportsmen show and model airplane contest drew 400,000 and 60,000 persons, respectively, during stays at Chapel Hill Mall.

Fig. 15--Example of recreation story. (Courtesy, The Goodyear Tire & Rubber Company)

111

Plant 1 starts 'waste watcher' program, plans 15 per cent scrap reduction in '73

Bob Pfister wants all Plant 1 employes to be "waste watchers."

Pfister, Plant 1 technical superintendent and chairman of a recently organized waste committee, said his group wants to reduce plant waste by at least 15 per cent for the remainder of 1973.

The committee was formed at the request of Howard Ginaven, Plant 1 manager.

"Our campaign will be geared to reduce waste of materials," he noted, "but control of scrap applies to all products."

Pfister outlined several points of his committee's plan to make war on waste.

"Defective areas on fabric tire parts are a great cause of waste," he explained. "Careful attention on the part of everyone who handles the fabric can help avoid such costly errors.

"We can keep the amount of scrap to a bare minimum by scrapping only the defective area and no more. Many times, much good material is thrown out with a bad portion.

"Over-runs of material also are very costly.

"The combined efforts of production, production control, quality control and development," Pfister pointed out, "can be aimed at reducing waste in the plant processes. This will cover all production areas—from the mixing of compounds through the curing of tires."

Other members of the committee are Bob Smyth, department foreman, calender room; Willard McDonald, shift foreman, cutters and band room; Ivan Coleman, manager of waste control; "Speed" Gaskins, department foreman, industrial tires, and Gene Griffey, department foreman, race tires.

Fig. 16--Example of waste story. (Courtesy, The Goodyear Tire & Rubber Company)

Improvements announced in basic medical benefits

Highlights of improvements in basic medical benefits for ALL Akron employes and retirees are announced

The basic plan provides company-paid protection against medical expenses for you and your dependents. The following improvements have been made in the basic plan, effective April 26:

1) Payment of charges for medical tests such as basal metabolism, electrocardiograph and electroencephalogram when performed in a physician's office. Previously such tests were covered only on a referral by the employe's doctor to a laboratory, hospital or another doctor's office.

2) Payment of charges for diagnostic laboratory tests wherever performed. Only exception under the revised plan is when a doctor operates the laboratory and only makes tests in connection with his own practice and does not make any tests for patients of other doctors.

3) Payment for radiation therapy
(Please turn to Page 4-5)

Fig. 17--Example of benefits story. Story continued on next page. (Courtesy, The Goodyear Tire & Rubber Company)

Basic medical benefits improved

(Continued from Page 1)

wherever performed. Previously such tests had to be performed in an outpatient department of a hospital.

4) Maximum amount payable for outpatient radiation therapy has been increased from $500 to $600 in a 12-consecutive month period.

5) Additional procedures are now included in the list of non-operative or specific therapeutic procedures paid as surgery when performed in lieu of surgery.

6) Payments for medical visits in a hospital are increased from $7 daily to $10 daily.

7) Payments for medical visits in a hospital also are payable during a subsequent confinement following surgery if such confinement is separated by a non-confinement period of at least seven days. (Example: A patient is released after a surgical confinement. About 10 days later complications develop from the original surgery and he returns to the hospital. In this case medical visits are paid for. Previously they were not.)

8) Coordination of benefits. Benefits of the revised basic program will be coordinated with the coverage a patient may have under other plans so that the total of all benefits will not exceed 100 per cent of eligible expenses. Purpose of the Goodyear program is to help meet the medical expenses that you actually incur. This new provision recognizes that some employes are protected under more than one program and provides for an adjustment of benefits so that the total benefits equal the actual expenses.

9) In cases where both the husband and wife are employed by Goodyear, either person will be considered as also being eligible for benefits as a dependent of their spouse. The wife, under the old plan, was covered only as a single individual with no dependents.

Complete details outlining the improved basic plan will appear in booklets to be distributed to all employes.

Fig. 17 (Continued)

THESE THREE PHOTOS, taken of tires on autos in the employe parking lot at Seiberling Field, are good examples of how not to start out on a vacation trip this summer. The tire at left checked out at 14 psi, about half the correct tire pressure. Marks on the sidewall indicate excessive sidewall flexing and potential failure. The tire in the center photo not only is underinflated but the wear bar indicates the tread has reached the 1/16th depth level—the minimum allowed by Ohio law. Smooth tires such as the one in the right photo are the latest thing in speedway racing but they have no place on the highway. Driving on a bald tire in Ohio is as illegal as speeding.

An eye on inflation can keep tire costs down

Fig. 18--Example of tire inflation feature. (Courtesy, The Goodyear Tire & Rubber Company)

CHAIRMAN Russell DeYoung (left photo, left) congratulates Winfield S. "Scotty" Chapman, a Los Angeles tire plant power truck operator, for winning the company's annual "Spirit Award" for outstanding company and community service. Chapman's wife, Marguerite, holds his $1,000 award check. Mr. and Mrs. Edwin J. Thomas (right photo), founders of the Goodyear Spirit Award, personally congratulate the Chapmans during an informal reception at the Thomas home following the formal presentation at the annual employe Christmas program in Goodyear Theater. The award is financed by the Thomas family. (Photos by Ron Stockwell)

Chapman: 'Spirit Award highlight of my life'

By RICK STEINLE
Wingfoot Clan Associate Editor

It didn't take Winfield S. "Scotty" Chapman long to tell a large crowd at the Goodyear Theater how he felt about receiving the 1972 Goodyear Spirit Award. "It's the highlight of my life," said the 63-year-old Chapman. "Definitely the highlight."

An inside power truck operator at the Los Angeles tire plant, Chapman was named the seventh winner of the Edwin J. and Mildred V. Thomas Spirit Award on Dec. 22. The award, financed by Thomas, former Goodyear chairman, and his wife, is given annually to an employe or retiree who demonstrates zeal, loyalty, dedication and human understanding. The award, a bronze medallion and a $1,000 check, is presented to the winner at the annual employe Christmas program.

Although Chapman made an eloquent acceptance speech, he had every right to be at a loss for words when Russell De-Young, board chairman, announced that "Scotty" was the Spirit Award recipient.

"We were told to come to Akron to receive the award for the tire manufacturing division," Chapman said. "It turned out that my wife, Marguerite, knew about the big award in advance," Chapman said after the presentation. "That's the first time in 41 years she hasn't told me the truth."

A native of Baton Rouge, La., Chapman moved to LA in the late 1920s and started at the company's plant there in May, 1942. He is the first Spirit Award winner to be selected under the contest's expanded, worldwide nominating system.

This year Goodyear honored more than 100 first-level Spirit Award winners at plants, offices, plantations and sales outlets across the country and around the world. From this number, 17 divisional winners were selected for the contest finals. A blue ribbon committee in Akron named the Spirit winner from the divisional finalists.

Besides being one of the best known and well respected employes at the LA plant, Chapman has established a remarkable record of community service. As a Shriner he has raised funds for the Los Angeles City of Hope Hospital and the Sickle Cell Anemia Fund. In 1971, Chapman was co-chairman of a successful AID (Associated In-Group Donors) Fund in his plant, a campaign similar to the United Fund drive at Goodyear-Akron.

A number of years ago, Chapman founded a boy's club in his neighborhood. "Scotty" still serves that group, called the Royal Knights, in addition to helping at a YMCA branch in the city. Chapman also is a member of the Urban League and is active in his Methodist Church's Boy Scout troop.

The capstone to Chapman's "public spiritedness" came in May, 1971, when the California State Assembly passed a resolution commending "Scotty" for his more than a quarter of a century of service to the Los Angeles community.

After receiving the award, Chapman and his wife visited the Thomases at their Akron home before returning to LA for Christmas. "I knew Goodyear was a closely-knit family but it's even more of one than I thought," Chapman said.

Chapman will receive a "Spirit Award spinoff" honor in two years when his trucker's work badge will be retired when he does. The badge will be plated in gold and given to Chapman when he leaves Goodyear.

Fig. 19--Example of employee recognition story. (Courtesy, The Goodyear Tire & Rubber Company)

ALTHOUGH FRED WOOD is confined to a wheelchair (left photo) after losing both legs because of circulation problems, he is a gardener who is up early each morning tending his flowers, shrubs and lawn at his Seminole, Fla., home. He also keeps busy (right photo) by helping his wife, Peggy, in her ceramics studio at the rear of their home. They are shown putting the finishing touches on lighted ceramic Christmas trees. Fred retired from Plant 1 build truck tires in 1962. At that time the doctor said he'd be dead in six months. (Photos courtesy of St. Petersburg (Fla.) Times and Evening Independent)

Plant 1 retiree still faces life with a twinkle

Circulatory problems required the amputation of one leg in 1970 and the other in 1971, but that hasn't stopped Fred Wood from keeping busy in his retirement years.

He and his wife, Peggy, are very active with their gardening and ceramics work at their home in Seminole, Fla. Fred retired from Plant 1 build truck tires in 1962. He had diabetes and his legs bothered him. The doctor said he'd be dead in six months.

Today—almost 11 years later—he sits in his wheelchair and rolls around his lawn weeding the flower beds. The lawn is smooth and bright green, and the roses, hibiscus and crotons sparkle with color and health.

The tanned retiree looks strong and healthy, not at all like a man of 72 who has lost both legs in the past three years.

"I can't keep up with my work," Fred says seriously. He seldom smiles, but there's usually a twinkle in his eyes.

Fred grew up in North Carolina, joined the Marines at 18 and served on the flagship of the European fleet until the end of World War I.

"I bummed around for a few years, then settled down in Ohio," he explains. "I went to work for Goodyear and was with the company 38 years—18 in truck tire building and 20 as a supervisor."

After retiring, he and Peggy lived with her mother in West Virginia. Then about three years ago they bought their home in Seminole.

"The yard was overgrown with large shrubs and weeds, and I've done all this myself," he says proudly. "After my legs were amputated I knew I had my mind straight and had two good arms, a lot more than a lot of fellows have. Before my second leg amputation was healed, I was out digging."

While Fred works outside, Peggy keeps busy inside. Together they built a small glass greenhouse (attached to their home) for a growing collection of orchids.

Peggy was a Goodyearite, too. That's where they met and married 25 years ago. Her hobby was ceramics. The pastime developed to the point that she left Goodyear and opened a studio where she taught ceramics.

"Many of my students were those sent by doctors," she says. "They needed therapy or rehabilitation. Ceramics should be used more widely in rehabilitation. Working with clay releases tensions.

"Fred was bedfast from 1962 to 1964 and he had lost most of his ability to use his hands. Then one day when he was feeling better he asked to go out to the studio. He began playing with clay, working his hands back and forth, and it helped him."

Peggy is an artist with ceramics. Many of the pieces she molds herself. The Woods' large back porch was converted to a studio when they moved there. Now the shelves that line the walls are crammed with molds and unfired ceramics.

Fred doesn't slow down until he's in his hospital-type bed for the night. A rod suspended from the ceiling allows him to move himself, and he can control the back rest on the bed. Then—and only then—he watches television.

The children on the street where they live are Fred's friends. "They call me 'Pop' when they go by," he says, as the twinkle appears in his eyes again.

Fig. 20--Example of employee recognition story. (Courtesy, The Goodyear Tire & Rubber Company)

It's little things that help conserve energy

By C. EDWARD FORD

Just by turning the thermostat down three degrees at Goodyear's Topeka plant, enough fuel could be saved during one winter to heat the home of an employe for 50 to 60 years.

"It's the little things that count where fuel conservation is concerned," according to Charles Hiss, Goodyear's manager of corporate engineering. "A lower thermostat setting, a door or window that's not left open, a light that's turned off when not needed . . . they all add up to a big saving in fuel consumption."

Fuel conservation is fast becoming a way of life for many industries because America, energy experts say, has reached the end of a long era in which low-cost energy was abundantly available. Now, the energy resources that enabled the nation to become the world's leading industrial power are rapidly dwindling.

Goodyear has been involved in fuel conservation programs for several years and

Board Chairman Russell DeYoung confirms that the conservation practices will continue (see accompanying statement).

Hiss noted that "the amount of energy we conserve will depend a great deal upon

(Please turn to Page 3)

Goodyear support pledged

The nation's natural energy sources — coal, oil and gas — provide the tremendous energy needed to turn the wheels of American industry and keep the economy moving forward.

Ever increasing demands for these vital elements by business, industry and the public sector make it more imperative than ever before that they are used efficiently and wisely. Moreover, exploration and development of additional energy supplies is not keeping pace with accelerating demands.

Fuel shortages can adversely affect the company's progress and the well-being of its employes and their families. Recognizing this crucial fact, Goodyear pledges to give the highest priority to fuel conservation, energy-saving techniques and the development of other energy sources, such as atomic power.

Russell De Young

Chairman of the Board

It's little things that help conserve energy

(Continued from Page 1)

the cooperation of employes. Each employe can contribute by doing such things as turning off lights and air conditioners when not needed. It also will help if air conditioners are operated at more conservative settings. And, next winter, we can save on fuel by keeping thermostats at moderate levels.

"During cold weather, it's particularly important to keep windows and doors closed," he emphasized. "This is especially true where some of our bigger loading doors are concerned."

Hiss said production employes can assist by making every attempt to reduce scrap as this will cut down on machine use.

"Also, we ask that they avoid the unnecessary use of compressed air, particularly for such things as cooling production equipment. And it's important to report to your supervisor such things as leaking faucets and water fountains that operate continuously. They not only waste water, but use excessive amounts of electricity through continuous pumping and refrigeration.

"And I hope employes also will contact their supervisors if they discover any leaks, bad valves or uninsulated pipes in the manufacturing or office areas."

Hiss said that while it was important for employes to practice fuel conservation at work, they also could help the overall energy conservation effort by practicing fuel conservation in their homes.

The corporate engineering department also has recommended a number of steps to be taken by each manufacturing facility.

"Beginning in 1971, we advised each of our plants to avoid potential energy shortages by giving close attention to the use of electricity, water, compressed air and steam," Hiss explained. "The immediate results of this action are lower energy use and cost.

Processes being reviewed

"We also have asked plant managers to review all production processes and reduce energy requirements to a minimum. To save on electrical power, we have suggested a reduction of peak energy demands through such things as staggering the startup on heavy equipment such as banburys, mills and calenders."

Proper maintenance of machines and equipment also can reduce energy usage, Hiss said.

"This means keeping heating, cooling, power and process equipment in top operating condition and checking for such things as steam leakage and poor pipe insulation," he added.

"During cold months, it will pay to turn down thermostats several degrees, particularly in areas that are not always occupied."

There is much speculation nationally about what lies ahead. The consensus among energy experts is that energy conservation is a must, but, regardless, it seems a certainty that bills for electricity, heating and gasoline will get even higher. Even severe rationing of these necessities is not inconceivable. In Florida, gallon limits already are being set on gasoline purchases. Gasoline shortages also have occurred in Massachusetts, Minnesota and Oregon, and in Akron, wholesalers are placing limits on gasoline supplied to service stations.

Sen. Henry Jackson, who is chairman of the Senate Committee on Interior and Insular Affairs and is considered an expert on energy matters, is graphic in his evaluation of the energy crisis.

"It's the most critical problem—domestic or international—facing the nation today," he said

Fig. 21--Example of energy conservation story. (Courtesy, The Goodyear Tire & Rubber Company)

All-fiberglass radial tires being made by Goodyear

Goodyear has revealed that it is supplying all fiberglass-reinforced radial tires to U.S. auto manufacturers for evaluation.

Three auto companies have been testing the new tires for more than a year and Goodyear is preparing to make them available in the replacement market in limited quantities, according to T.M. Kersker, director of tire textile development.

Fiberglass has been used for some time in the belts of bias-belted tires, like Goodyear's Polyglas tire marketed since 1967, but not in the main body cords of tires actually put on the market.

The new Goodyear radial tire has fiberglass cords in the body as well as in the belts.

The all glass and rubber construction provides long durability, a smooth ride, improved handling and other benefits, according to Kersker.

"On a weight basis, glass reinforcement is stronger than steel, a factor which will permit designs that will result in better fuel economy," he said.

Fig. 22--Example of new product story. (Courtesy, The Goodyear Tire & Rubber Company)

Akron labor-management agreement 'provides basis for some optimism'

A new labor-management agreement covering Akron plants "provides the basis for some optimism toward Goodyear's goal of making plants here competitive with those throughout the rest of the country."

This view was expressed by Vice President O.M. Sherman after some 1,800 members of Local 2-United Rubber Workers last Sunday ratified a supplemental agreement to the company-wide master contract.

"The changes agreed to in the supplement represent a significant effort to improve the operating effectiveness of the Akron plants," Sherman said. "The cooperative efforts by Local 2 will help the company maintain the employment level in Akron.

"The company will continue to seek ways to make the Akron operations as efficient and competitive as possible. It is looking forward to the continuing cooperation of Local 2 in maintaining as full employment as possible in the Akron plants, in addition to providing continuing job opportunities in this area."

Sherman also pointed out that the agreement will enable the company to obtain increased effectiveness from crafts employes. The cooperative attitude of the skilled craftsmen will make it possible to effect some significant cost savings, he said.

It is the first time in memory that Local 2 (or any URW local) and the company had agreed on a supplement prior to agreement on a master contract.

John Nardella, president of Local 2 and the union's chief negotiator, said ratification of the supplemental agreement "shows that we are willing to accept change, if it means keeping jobs here. We made concessions we never did make before and we made them for the sake of keeping jobs in Akron."

Among the changes in the Akron agreement are these:

1) Cancellation of the three-day "hold-up" period currently allowed the union to consider new or revised piecework rates which otherwise would take effect immediately. The new agreement allows new rates to become effective immediately.

2) Reduction in the number of skilled trades classifications. Riggers and boilermakers will be absorbed into the repairman classification and tinner-welders will be absorbed into the welder classification.

3) For the efficient utilization of manpower, a skilled trades employe may be assigned work in another classification for short periods of time (up to one-half hour) when the work is incidental to the primary assignment and is within the employe's capabilities.

4) The Plant 2 janitor service and transportation balancing groups will be split out with current work station and job line-up agreements to remain unchanged within each group. This provision covers tires, reclaim and industrial products.

5) Upon his request an employe may receive one week vacation in lieu of time off in addition to the week already provided in the master contract. This is designed to reduce overtime payments to employes working longer hours filling in for vacationing employes.

6) An employe may not bid on a vacancy until he has attained two years of service. Formerly he had to have one year of service.

7) Changes were made in provisions

(Please turn to Page 2)

Agreement

(Continued from Page 1)

covering distribution of work, and in job bidding and bumping.

8) Wash-up time and clothing allowances were provided in certain areas.

9) Changes were made in wage rates in several areas.

10) If feasible, pay checks for bargaining unit employes will be inserted in envelopes. (Feasibility means whether the company can insert the checks in envelopes and still get them out in time. Bargaining unit employes are paid weekly.)

The effective date of the Akron agreement will be determined by the effective date of the master contract, which expires April 20. Negotiations on this contract begin Monday in Cincinnati.

The Akron negotiations were the culmination of discussions that have been carried on over a two-year period. Heading the company team in these talks was James A. Culler, personnel manager, Akron plants.

Fig. 23--Example of labor contract story. (Courtesy, The Goodyear Tire & Rubber Company)

118

Goodyear named one of nine companies helping Vietnam prisoners get new jobs

Goodyear is going to help Vietnam prisoners of war get jobs either with the company or elsewhere.

The company is one of nine major manufacturers on a Pentagon-appointed Industry Committee on POW Employment. Others on the committee are five service industries and two professional organizations.

The committee will serve as a clearing house in offering repatriated veterans the broadest possible choice of civilian employment opportunities.

"We plan to make every effort to assure employment for any POW who is interested in leaving the Armed Forces and entering civilian life," said O.M. Sherman, vice president of industrial relations.

Job offers to those servicemen now returning to the States are "innumerable," the Pentagon has indicated, and no difficulty is expected in absorbing them into the civilian economy.

Each of the 16 committee members is responsible for at least one of the 31 military hospitals to which the POWs are being assigned.

Goodyear is responsible for funneling job offers and arranging interviews for the 18 POWs and 52 MIAs assigned to Fort Gordon Army Hospital, Augusta, Ga. (MIAs are those originally listed as missing in action.)

Here's how the system works:

A U.S. Employment counselor is stationed at each hospital. Veterans ready to seek employment contact the counselor for information on all companies offering jobs. In the case of Fort Gordon, Goodyear is contacted by the counselor after the veteran expresses an interest in particular companies. Goodyear then arranges with those companies to send interviewers to Fort Gordon immediately.

The Goodyear contact and committee member is Robert A. Morris of sales personnel.

When the Pentagon invited Goodyear and the others to form the committee last November, it listed at that time 587 prisoners of war and 1,329 missing in action in Southeast Asia.

The count on the POWs has been revised slightly since then to 570 in both North and South Vietnam, but the status of those missing in action is still unclear.

Assisting the committee are the Department of Labor's U.S. Employment Service and the National Committee-Jobs for Veterans.

Fig. 24--Example of corporate image story. (Courtesy, The Goodyear Tire & Rubber Company)

MIKE CHARLEY (left) and John Lechman give Mike's grandchildren some experienced pointers and pushes on the shuffleboard courts at Wingfoot Lake Park. Mike works in Plant 3 shipping. The action took place during the Fourth of July holiday.

JUST HOLDING ON can be a real task when the merry-go-round starts picking up steam. Wingfoot Lake's spinner got a real workout last week as hundreds of families visited the park over the Fourth of July holiday. One of the benefits of the park's playground is the soft rubber "carpeting" that takes the "ouch" out of falls.

A MAN-SIZED YELL from two-year-old Harry Duh (left) marked the beginning of a quick ride down the sliding board with his brother, Elia. Harry and Elia, 8, are the sons of Ben Duh, fiber technical center, and were just two of many youngsters using the park playground during the holidays.

FISHWORMS are supposed to scare girls, but fisherwoman Julie Gleisinger hasn't heard that yet. She's baiting up before trying her luck in the park lagoon. Julie is the niece of Joseph Gleisinger, Plant 2 powerhouse.

July Fourth holidays lured many to Wingfoot Lake

Story By Fred Haymond, Photos By Rick Steinle

Winter and spring rains may have kept the corn below traditional knee-high-by-the-Fourth-of-July height, but last week's bright skies and warm temperatures brought many Goodyearites into the outdoors—especially to Wingfoot Lake.

While the children's fishing pond was covered with bright red "bobbers" attached to a variety of cane poles, the lake itself was a hodgepodge of rowboats. Some of the small craft were powered by motors, but most were pulled through the water by not-so-sure hands on oars.

The kids, for the most part, stared at their lines in hopes of snaring a gullible bluegill or sunfish, but many of the adults could be seen lounging in their boats apparently concerned only with how to catch a little more sun.

The rubberized playground was given a real workout by the younger set. More than one small body bounced off the sliding boards, teeter-totters or swings. With a rubber carpet for a landing pad, most of the bounces ended with smiles instead of tears.

With dad trying to land a record bass or a little tan and the kids mesmerized by the playground equipment, mom usually was left with the picnic duties.

More than a few moms apparently decided to let the chores go until the family returned. Many just sat in the cool breeze and read or napped or watched.

Just like Fourths gone by and Fourths of the future—the 1973 holiday was a nice time to be with the family.

EVEN SHOELACES can be the center of attraction for a two-year-old. Beth Gleisinger, another niece of Plant 2's Joseph Gleisinger, thought her laces were the greatest things going. While her relatives wet their fishing lines in the lake, Beth was content to sit by a tackle box and count the blessings of a loose lace.

JOHN CONLEY, 13, picked his own private spot from which to fish during a visit last week to Wingfoot Lake. John's father, Philip, works at GAC. More than a few lines were wetted during the two-day Fourth of July holiday.

STEAKS were on the picnic menu for the Chuck Berger family after a full morning of relaxation and recreation. Chuck, of Goodyear Aerospace, handles the cooking chores while the rest of the family awaits the call for "soup's on!"

MARK LEE (right) holds the fish while his dad, Donald Lee, and brother, Bruce, view the catch. The Lees took advantage of the mild July 4 weather to haul in bluegill and sunfish from the lake. Don is a Plant 2 tire builder.

The Wingfoot Clan—July 12, 1973—Page 3

Fig. 25--Example of picture page. (Courtesy, The Goodyear Tire & Rubber Company)

Inflation, unions among topics covered in survey

A nationwide survey consisting of more than 2,500 interviews and undertaken by a nationally-known research firm reveals attitudes of the public and union members toward inflation, unions and other issues.

The survey was conducted by Opinion Research Corporation (ORC) of Princeton, N.J., in November and December, 1972, and the findings were just made public. Among the 2,500 interviews were more than 500 with pensioners or other elderly persons living on fixed incomes.

Highlights of the survey, according to ORC, show the following:

*The public is more prone to blame government than either business or labor when placing responsibility for inflation.

*About one in four persons feels that companies can somehow accommodate wage increases without raising prices.

*One out of every three union members feels that the government should "put pressure" on unions to hold down wage demands.

*Almost two out of every three persons feel that unions should be closely regulated by the government, despite the fact that the public seems less concerned about labor power and unrest today than any year since 1964.

*Six in 10 say wages paid in the U.S. make it difficult for American products to compete in world markets.

*Seventy per cent feel that union leaders today are doing an unsatisfactory job in meeting their responsibilities to the public at large. In 1970, the figure was 60 per cent. Among union members, the increase was from 53 per cent in 1970 to 69 per cent in 1972.

*About four out of five persons feel there should be a law that guarantees union members the right to criticize their leaders without being disciplined by the union.

*Eighty-six per cent of union members and 83 per cent of the public favor secret ballots before strike decisions are made. A similar question in 1955 showed 76 per cent of union members, and 81 per cent of the public, favored such a proposal.

*About 46 per cent of the public, the same percentage as in 1971, feel that welfare benefits should not be provided to striking workers. Forty per cent think they should. Among the general public, 53 per cent feel that strikers should not be entitled to welfare benefits because "they are out of work by their own choice."

*The public is just about evenly divided, according to the survey, on the argument that getting welfare and food stamps is a matter of right for any needy person and should not matter whether the person is on strike or not.

*Although willing to let public employes join unions, the majority of the general public is opposed to virtually all types of strikes in essential service industries.

*Among union members, majorities are against strikes for the armed forces, police, firemen, hospital employes and prison guards.

*Of those who expressed an opinion, a larger majority of pensioners than the general public (79 per cent vs. 62 per cent) feels the government should put pressure on unions to hold down wage demands.

*Two-thirds of both the public and union members favor a law that permits management to discipline employes who become involved in labor violence. Both percentages have grown since 1966.

Fig. 26--Example of survey story. (Courtesy, The Goodyear Tire & Rubber Company)

THEY MAY LOOK GOOD to the untrained eye, but these tires are useless. Leonard Boso, classifier in industrial and small airplane tires, daily stacks rejected tires in large boxes. Each of the tires, for a variety of reasons, is no good and must be discarded. About $13,000 in tires is wasted each month from just the industrial and small airplane tire lines.

$13,000 lost per month

Scrap tires costing Plant 1

A scrap tire is like a clock with no hands. It's useless.

Bob Pfister, Plant 1 technical superintendent, estimates $13,000 is wasted each month in just the industrial and small airplane tires department. That $13,000 is down the drain as the tires cannot be salvaged in any way.

Pfister, chairman of the Plant 1 waste control committee, wants to decrease the number of scrap tires that come off each line each day.

"The company has to pay to have the scrap hauled away, just like any other trash," he explained.

"The most common reasons for defects," said Pfister, "are improper setup of equipment when a mold is changed, blows due to trapped air and improper application of precure paint and inside lining cements."

Some tires can be repaired or buffed, but even in those cases there is a waste of man-hours. Workers who could be making tires must spend part of their time repairing defective ones.

"Alert employes doing their jobs thoroughly and correctly can be a tremendous help in cutting waste," said Pfister.

He suggested these ways to prevent scrap:

BUILD TIRES properly with no air or foreign material in them. Oil, grease and paper in the tire can make it defective.

MAINTAIN PROPER coverage of precure paint and lining cement.

CHECK CURING equipment to assure it is set and operating correctly. If there are any problems, contact a supervisor.

MAKE SURE the proper tire is being put into each mold.

Fig. 27--Example of waste story. (Courtesy, The Goodyear Tire & Rubber Company)

Fig. 28--Example of story from publication tailored for salaried employees. (Courtesy, The Goodyear Tire & Rubber Company)

Mayor Stevic ponders a point during a village council meeting. He attends 18 to 20 evening meetings each month, leaving little free time for himself and his family.

Leading a double life

The ups outweigh downs for mayor of Mogadore

This is the main intersection of Mogadore, a community that has so caught Don Stevic's affections that he has served it in public office for more than a decade. The Chemical Division foreman is mayor of the village.

Don Stevic's normally placid features registered shock and dismay as he put down the phone.

"You think that doesn't shake you up," gasped the 49-year-old Chemical Division department foreman, "when the Beacon Journal calls to tell you you're being sued for $50,000."

Stevic leads a double life. By day he supervises a production department at Plant 1 that makes Goodyear Pliolite bases and resins used in paint manufacture. But in the evenings and on weekends he is transformed into an active public servant in the suburban village of Mogadore, a role that has carried him through three terms as a village councilman, four terms as mayor and smack into a lawsuit that hasn't yet been resolved.

The suit is one of five filed by a former village employe against Stevic and four councilmen after they cast votes that resulted in his ouster for what they viewed as improper conduct on the job. The legal action marks the low point in a 13-year career as a local politician for Stevic. But to him the

Fig. 29--Example of employee recognition story from publication for salaried employees. Story continues on next two pages. (Courtesy, The Goodyear Tire & Rubber Company)

years have held more ups than downs.

He can tick off a long list of village improvements made during his terms on the council and in the mayor's office. During the past decade, the village police department has grown from three men to a force of five full-time officers and nine part-timers. The fire department has replaced two old trucks with modern pumpers, street lights have been converted to modern, mercury vapor lamps, storm and sanitary sewers have been laid throughout the village and its 13½ miles of streets now are all hard surfaced.

"My biggest satisfaction was passage of a payroll income tax that permitted us to reduce property tax collections by one third," Stevic said.

Mogadore is a tranquil community of 4,825, known to many Akron area residents as the site of a reservoir that offers top bass and panfish angling. During the past 18 years, Stevic and his wife have raised a family of three there.

In 1959, he ran for a two-year term on the village council, following that with election to a four-year term in 1961. In January, 1962, he was named president of the council, becoming acting mayor six months later.

In February, 1963, after the death of Mayor Robert Faulkner, also a Goodyear employe, Stevic was designated to serve out the term. In November

Beneath one of the modern, mercury vapor lamps that now illumine the streets of Mogadore, mayor Don Stevic, left, and council president Don Roepke, a Goodyear Aerospace employe, compare notes before a village council meeting.

Fig. 29 (Continued)

of that year he was elected to the first of two consecutive two-year terms as mayor. In 1967, Stevic was beaten at the polls and reluctantly retired from public life until November, 1969, when he was once again elected to council. He won as mayor again in November, 1971.

Why is Stevic driven to run for office again and again? It's not the money. The offices pay only a meager sum; and people sue him.

"I guess I do it because I care about the community " he observed. "I don't want to see it revert back to a one-horse town.

"I think everybody ought to get their feet wet at least once in their life. You shouldn't complain about government until you've sat in the seat and seen what's going on.

"One of the biggest problems is that people don't understand how government works. If they'd take time to learn more about how it operates, they might be happier with how their tax dollars are spent.

"The only way you can learn is to get involved."

Twice each month, on the first and third Wednesday evenings, Don Stevic walks into Mogadore's municipal building to preside over council meetings. Other than that, his schedule includes mayor's court, traffic court, committee sessions and community meetings.

In a normal month he attends 18 to 20 meetings, which may win him popularity with Mogadore voters, but don't get him many points with his wife.

"She thinks I've done my share," he said, "and she'd rather I'd spend more time at home.

"But she does back me on some of my policies."

What about the policies that don't win Mrs. Stevic's support?

"On those," the mayor concluded, "she tells me what she thinks of them."

Stevic chats with Mogadore fire chief Larry Pettit. The new pumper, right, replaced the older 1946 model, left, in 1971.

Fig. 29 (Continued)

tire center overcomes the unexpected

waves of progress in atlanta

By Mike Starn

CAN A RESPECTED, successful black real estate salesman also make waves in the tire business with an all-black staff in a predominantly black neighborhood?

The obvious answer is yes.

The real answer is no, then yes.

For the answer to that answer, GO Magazine talked with Allen Caldwell, the real estate salesman mentioned above, new dealer in Goodyear tires and old dealer in the incongruities of life.

Caldwell is majority owner of Caldwell & Sykes Inc., a Goodyear franchise tire center in the West End section of Atlanta.

West End is a transition neighborhood, and, like many other such neighborhoods across the country, that means whites are moving out and blacks are moving in. Not in droves, just a home here, an apartment there.

A sweet situation for a black businessman, right? Wrong.

Though Caldwell has handled real estate for both black and white Atlantans for the past 20 years, he was not prepared for the type of reception he received when the former Goodyear service store on Ashby St. became a minority owned tire center two years ago.

"We were searching for a good, dependable business that everyone respected and that carried a product with nationwide acceptance," Caldwell recalls. "We went over a long list of possibilities, attended quite a few trade shows, but at first couldn't settle on one we wanted to go with.

"Then I saw the Goodyear franchise tire center ad in the Wall Street Journal, and the idea appealed to me immediately. We touched base with the Goodyear people, attended a number of conferences, and later decided that this was the course for us."

As a Goodyear retail operation, the store had a succession of managers over the past 16 years, all white. The last manager had been Bill Wilson, a savvy salesman and tight organizer who had brought the store solidly into the profit column, and who now manages an equally successful store in another Atlanta suburb.

The customer mix was about the same then as now—about 70 per cent black. The logical conclusion to be drawn, and one which Caldwell and nephew Clarence Sykes no doubt drew, was that if Wilson, a white, had done that well, then a black businessman would do even better.

"Not so," Caldwell says. "A white person may

Fig. 30--Example of dealer recognition story in dealer magazine. Story continues on next three pages. (Goodyear Tire & Rubber Company)

Allen Caldwell encountered a surprise reaction when he became a partner in a tire center.

Fig. 30 (Continued)

have difficulty understanding it, because whites for the most part are unaware of the subtleties of white/black association over the years.

"You would probably think that blacks would not hesitate to trade with blacks, no matter what the circumstances; that they would be glad to do it, just because the business is black owned and operated. But that wasn't the case. At first, we handled much of the same trade that had dealt regularly with the service store, but after word got around that the operation was wholly black, our trade dropped off measurably. And it was the blacks who wouldn't deal with us."

Caldwell explained that much of the difficulty

Fred Anderson, store manager, feels the key to running a good tire center is being yourself, talking to your customers and leveling with them.

Caldwell (above) says that operating a tire center is time-consuming, hard, dirty work, but "the satisfactions are many." At left, Fred Anderson and a Fulton County Airport employe check out landing gear on a small plane. Caldwell and Sykes supplies tires and tubes to the busy airport. Clarence Skyes (right) handles the center's sizable budget business. "There is a great need in this buy-now-pay-later country," he says, "for people to be educated in the whys and wherefores of credit."

Fig. 30 (Continued)

came in dealing with older generation blacks who themselves had had less education, less training, less opportunity to become skilled in vocations formerly held mostly by whites.

"Therefore," he added, "there was no reason why they would feel that another black was qualified to give them the best service or that he knew what he was doing or what he was talking about. I remember one black woman, who, when she found out that we owned the store, told me to my face that she didn't deal with blacks and walked right out. I followed her out and told her I was shocked that she would feel that way. She promptly told me that it had always been that way and that's the way

she wanted it."

Where did they go from there?

"The only direction we could go," said Fred Anderson, store manager and former credit sales manager with Bill Wilson. "We had to start building the business again from the ground up. It was a slow but necessary process, but it worked, even against that kind of built-in attitude. We found that by talking to people, being yourself, and selling the Goodyear product that people had come to respect in this area, our trade began to grow again."

"We have overcome that old feeling now," Caldwell added, "and I think the younger generation had a lot to do with it. Blacks are a definite economic group now. The younger people want the Goodyear product and the service to go with it, no matter who's standing across the counter from them."

Over the months Caldwell, Anderson and Sykes, who is credit sales manager, have assembled a capable crew of sales and servicemen. This, Caldwell says, has been the spark the company needed. Documentary proof of that fact was the company's number one standing in the Southern Region in brake and alignment sales for two bays.

In one month's time, from two bays, two men pumped nearly $6,000 in B & A work into the company coffers.

"We're gradually putting together a good team here," said Caldwell. "Anyone who has ever been in this business will tell you it's tough to find good people, not because the talent isn't around but because so many of them just don't want to work. But through trial and error we've got a nucleus of people who know what they're doing, and they're good at conveying that impression to the public."

"Look at it this way," Anderson added. "We're right in the middle of a commercial area; we're surrounded by competitors, including the specialty shops who claim they can do a better job for you because they can concentrate on one problem point. But they're still not giving the service or their customers wouldn't be coming here."

Even a quick glance around the neighborhood will tell the visitor that West End is not a high income area. The bread winner punches a clock, carries a lunch pail and buys so-called luxury items on credit. But he also is a consumer and expects the kind of treatment the army of American consumer advocates tells him he should be getting. He is a bargain hunter and carefully plots the course of every dime, but is fiercely loyal to people he can trust.

"We've got that going for us too," Caldwell said. "We don't try to take advantage of anybody."

Fig. 30 (Continued)

Chapter

13

SETTING THE BUDGET

The budget—the amount of money available—is a crucial factor in deciding certain things about the publication.

The size of the budget, ultimately, will be decided by the comptroller, treasurer, or whoever has charge of authorizing spending.

This means probably there will be a proposed budget submitted to the company officials. After the comptroller and other officials have examined the proposal and possibly made revisions, the publication department will work from the approved budget. This could be larger, but probably will be smaller, than the proposed one.

(As has been pointed out in other chapters, the procedures will vary from company to company. In a small organization, the editor handles the whole job and then some. In large companies, there may be a large staff producing several publications aimed at several audiences. In this case, a lot of the detail work, as listed below, will be handled by a director of publications rather than the editor.)

The first step in setting up a budget will be to decide the various aspects of publishing. The proposal should designate the

BUDGET ALLOCATION CHART

	Paper	Printing	Engraving	Photos	Mailing	Postage	Circ.
Jan. 866.00	87.00	493.00	85.00	53.00	67.00	81.00	3300
Feb. 900.77	88.95	504.05	87.13	57.21	77.28	86.25	3353
Mar. 945.51	89.55	505.45	93.17	77.40	83.27	91.77	3523
Apr.							
May							
June							
July							

132

publication's format, frequency, page number, page size, printing method, grade of paper, number of colors to use, the press run, and circulation method.

The editor should list each of the expense items and costs, such as paper, mailing (if it is to be mailed), printing, photographs, etc.

The next step is to contact three potential suppliers for each of the expense items and get three written bids.

After the bids have been received, the editor should examine the shops of the suppliers, get samples of the work if appropriate, and talk to some of the suppliers' customers, ascertaining the quality of work and service. It is also appropriate to note the location of each supplier, and the condition of the shop and equipment. The editor should observe the work force and try to gauge whether his job will be handled with care and consideration or if there is less attention to the customers' needs.

All other factors being equal, the editor should choose a supplier who is the shortest distance away. Physical appearances oftentimes will provide hints. For instance, a clean, orderly shop with neat-appearing employees will usually produce a better quality work than a dirty, dingy shop staffed by sloppy employees.

In the case of the printer, it is imperative that the editor know what sizes of publication the printer can produce, what type of composition is used, and what type sizes are available in headline and body type.

The editor should find out if the printer has the potential

133

to do color printing. He also should learn what other auxiliary services can be provided, such as staff artists to do color separations, a department to handle mailing, etc.

In an organization big enough to produce a company publication, supplies and services will be bought by a purchasing agent. The editor should work closely with this individual in seeking bids, drawing up specifications, and awarding bids. It is the purchasing agent's job to save the company money by buying goods and services as cheaply as possible, as long as goods and services are of the desired standard.

The purchasing agent probably is not expert in printing, so he will have to trust the editor's judgment in choosing the proper supplier. If the printer with the lowest bid is unacceptable, the editor should be able to give sound reasons why the shop is unsatisfactory. An example might be that the printer cannot produce the desired page size, or that a poll of his customers proved the printer frequently fails to meet deadlines.

The editor's decision for choosing a supplier should never be based on emotion, relationship, or friendship. Such a choice will brand him as unprofessional, and therefore detrimental to the company.

The editor must keep in mind that the company has made a study of the need for the publication. Probably, on the basis of that study, the organization has already allocated a specific sum for the publication. If the editor habitually spends considerably more than budgeted, the company might stop publishing because it cannot afford the program.

For this reason, the editor should take care to control the budget, once the money has been approved. He should make certain that each bid is submitted in writing and that the contract states specifically how much money is to be spent for the specific product or service. One very good method of allocation is to split the yearly budget into the number of times the publication is to appear. For example, if the company allocated $12,000 per year for a monthly, the editor could budget $1,000 for each issue.

All copy for a publication must be cleared or approved in manuscript form before the material is marked and sent to the printer. It is up to the editor to tell management it is expensive to make changes after material has been set into composition.

It is best to write material to fit a previously designated space laid out on a rough dummy, so that the editor can avoid sending the printer more copy and art than is needed to fill the publication.

The printer should be informed that the publication is the only job to be handled under the contract. In this way the editor makes sure no one else in the organization will accidentally, or on purpose, run another job through the print shop on the editor's contract.

Further, the editor should have it firmly understood by all suppliers that his contract does not cover work produced by anyone else except the editor or his agent.

It should be kept in mind that the printer is no mind reader. All body copy should be clearly marked to show the type size and family to use, and the pica measure on which the material is to be set.

It is a matter of policy in print shops to "follow copy even if it goes out the window." This means the way the copy reads is the way the copy is set. Even misspellings are set on the assumption the editor purposely misspelled the word.

Each picture should be properly cropped and scaled to the desired size. On the flip side, outside the area to be engraved, the editor should designate what size, in picas, to engrave the picture. Each picture should be identified by name of publication. There should be a designation as to what line screen the picture should be engraved.

Each piece of copy and art should be fully identified so it does not get lost, and it must be marked with a complete set of lucid instructions. Indicated sizes of printing should be designated in picas, especially if the material is to be set in a job shop.

The job shop usually has many jobs in production at any given time. There is a great variety possible in the pica measure of columns from job to job. Therefore, the line measure should not be designated in columns, but in picas. The individual compositor is not expected to know what specific number of picas there are in the width of a particular customer's columns. Therefore, the designation of picas should be specific.

The editor should set definite deadlines for getting his material to the supplier and then should abide by those deadlines. There may be many times when he has to work overtime or take the work home with him to have material ready for the printer ahead of the deadline. If the editor is late with his copy, the shop will shove his job to the back of the job file. If the editor, even though late, still insists the printer keep his deadline, it may force the printer to work overtime. The editor will be charged accordingly.

It is especially bad to keep the printer waiting for final approval of the job while the publication sits on the press. If there is an unavoidable delay in getting copy to the printer or obtaining final approvals, the printer should be called immediately, rather than being kept in the dark.

The editor should make sure the quality of his work is top-drawer. Copy that is dirty (with several penciled corrections or strikeovers) should be retyped so it does not take a lot of time to set composition.

By the same token, all art must be of good quality so the engraver does not have to do extra work to get good reproductions. All glossies should have the same tonal quality. Otherwise, the engraver will have to spend extra time to make sure the prints are of good quality.

Any author's corrections should be avoided after copy has been set into composition because such changes cost the editor money.

The editor should avoid showy or ultra-expensive printing and engraving. Again, when he has extras done by the printer or engraver, it raises costs. Because most company publications entail a short press run, this means the cost is amortized over a few thousand copies. Expensive color work or other special work by the print shop can be easily justified if the publication has a press run of a half million or so. With the short press run of an industrial publication, the per-copy cost for such extra work can cut sharply into the editor's rather limited budget.

Probably the best way for the industrial editor to make maximum use of his budget is to stick to basic good editing and simple, readable layouts. Of course, color and other special effects can be used from time to time for specific purposes, such as a Christmas or anniversary issue. However, it is good to make sure that, if extra money is spent on one issue, less money is spent on a subsequent issue or two. The editor should make sure he does not habitually overspend the budget by a significant amount.

If he has overspent on one issue, he can save money on subsequent issues to bring the budget back into line by cutting the print order, reducing the number of pages, using fewer photographs, and mailing fewer copies. (See Budget Allocation Chart, page 132.)

The best way to guarantee the publication will be produced efficiently is to have an editor who knows his business work with a printer who knows his business.

CREATING AND ADAPTING FEATURES

Whether the company publication has a magazine or a newspaper format, the items carried in its columns will rarely class as news in the parlance of the daily newspaper.

Spot news is the prompt reporting of a timely event. Since most company publications appear weekly, semi-monthly, or monthly, there is little chance their columns will contain anything timely. Added to this is the fact that the production schedule of a house journal usually calls for three days to a week in the print shop. Then, too, there are the vital clearances of material, copy, and pictures. All of these steps take time and militate against speed in production.

Therefore, instead of spot news, company publications typically use feature stories. Almost every item will be a story about some created or contrived event.

Of course, there are a few minor, partially timely events, such as non-company honors given to employees or their families. There are deaths of employees or retirees. There are, possibly, uncontrolled events, such as explosions, fires, floods, etc., which fall under the category of timely news. However, those items significant enough for coverage in the public press will have been so reported days or weeks before the company publication has a chance to carry a story.

This means that stories lend themselves to a feature style, as opposed to the inverted pyramid format so common in the daily newspaper.

The first guide for the company publication editor in creating features is in the objectives or goals. For example, if one goal is employee recognition, the editor has to ferret out stories which pay tribute to employees' contributions to the company's success. Thus, if an employee does an exceptional job of quality control, scrap reduction, sales, etc., here is an excellent chance for an employee recognition feature story.

If one of the publication goals is the reduction of absenteeism, the editor should develop features about this topic. The best way is to write stories about employees who are faithful in attendance.

To carry the description a step further, it is always best for the desired company message to come in the words of the employee rather than in the words of management. For example, if one of the organization goals is support for the annual United Fund charities drive, the editor should avoid trying to sell the concept by depending upon management editorials and preachment. Instead, he should use the following procedure: Go through the company records and learn which employees have given strong support to United Fund in past fund raising campaigns. The next step is to interview those employees for their feelings concerning the good points of United Fund drives and why the United Fund gets their strong support. In other words, the editor should always accent the positive and keep in mind that the message is accepted more readily if it comes from an individual's peers rather than from management.

Of course, management should communicate with employees and other publics, because this is desirable. For example, in stories about the company's economic outlook, it is best to quote directly from management. In stories about company expansions, new products, etc., management is the best source of stories. But the editor should not forget the principle that people are more likely to give credence to the views of their peers than they are to a management source.

In creating events to report, the editor should work closely with the public relations department. If there is no public relations department or if the editor also doubles as the public relations man, he must work virtually alone in dreaming up situations to report.

In planning events and finding ideas for features, the editor must make a thorough study of the organization and learn the potential news sources.

One of these is the production department. The manager has records to show when the first item was produced and the current production pace. Therefore, the manager can predict with a great degree of accuracy when specific milestones will occur. For example, the production man might be able to say that, if our present pace continues, next year at this time our organization will have produced its 50-millionth unit.

Because the editor can predict an occurrence with a certain amount of accuracy, he can prepare this feature and the supporting pictures months in advance.

Another top source of information is the comptroller or treasurer. This individual has his fingers on all spending for the entire organization. He can tell the editor with great certainty what spending programs have been approved.

Many organizations have one person who has charge of group insurance and benefits programs. This individual can be of invaluable help to the editor in supplying figures about the amount of money spent for fringe benefits, hospitalization, surgery, retirement, etc.

The chief engineer or top civil engineer can feed the editor such statistics as how much electricity and water the organization uses in a given period. It is a simple matter from the facts supplied to come up with a meaningful story, with illustrations, to depict the amount of water used--a picture of a lake or of Niagara Falls, for example.

The editor should never overlook the possibilities of a research study as a fruitful source of feature stories. A simple questionnaire administered to the organization's employees should prove a gold mine of information and form the basis of feature stories for months to come. The editor should seek the advice of someone versed in polling before carrying out a study. The questionnaire should be given to all employees, and the editor should keep a check list to make sure every employee has completed one.

The actual administering of the form probably should be done by the supervisors. Each supervisor should be thoroughly briefed on the procedure before the study starts.

Such a questioning, properly conducted, will uncover a surprising amount of information pertaining to employee hobbies and community activities. The typical organization probably will discover that quite a few of its employees are holding municipal and county political jobs in their spare time. The company might find several of its employees serving as small-town mayors, firemen, and policemen. There are almost certain to be several leisure-time Protestant ministers on the payroll. Added to these will be a heavy sprinkling of scoutmasters, church deacons, school board members, Sunday school teachers, and others.

It sometimes comes as a surprise to an organization that some of its employees are entrepreneurs in their own right, off the job.

All of these activities and others are grist for the mill to help the editor prepare stories of employee recognition.

In the search for ideas, the editor should ferret out every possible source. In addition to calling on certain offices periodically, it is a good idea to keep a constant search for ideas from as many of the employees as possible. A wise editor will visit with employees at random and draw them out for possible story ideas.

The fertile brain of the editor, himself, should be able to think up literally thousands of ideas which will fit into the blueprint of the company's objectives. Most of these ideas will involve variations on the same theme. The editor has to tell the story again, again, and again, always bringing in a fresh approach.

Another extremely fruitful source of ideas is in the pages of other similar publications. Therefore, the editor should make it a point to have his name put on the mailing list of several dozen other publications. At least some of these journals should be from companies which face problems similar to the ones his company faces. For example, if the company makes steel, the editor should exchange publications with several steel-making companies. Occasionally, from reading other publications, an editor will be able to adapt an idea for use in his publication. Bear in mind that no one is smart or original enough to have all of the ideas. All great authors of history have borrowed ideas from peers or authors of an earlier time.

Many large companies give an assist to their editors in sub-sidiary plants and divisions by furnishing idea sheets and by suggesting that each editor put every other editor in the organization on his mailing list.

In organizations which are large enough to have a news bureau as well as an internal publication, the company usually has some arrangement whereby the editor receives a copy of each news release. This also is a fruitful source of ideas. Although the publication cannot be timely in its treatment of such releases, the editor often is given a lead which he can develop into a feature. Of course, the company publication would give the story a company slant. This means the editor would give much interpretation explaining what this latest announcement would mean to the employees. This is the type of interpretation which could not be written into a release going to daily papers, radio stations, and magazines.

A flood of adaptable materials can be obtained from the Red Cross, National Safety Council, American Medical Association, Boy Scouts, Girl Scouts, National Chamber of Commerce, United Funds of America, and dozens of other sources. Each of these organizations prepares feature stories by the dozens to supply the needs of company publications. The organizational editor should be on the mailing lists of these organizations because, occasionally, the editor may be able to adapt an idea from one of these sources.

Another source is the North American Precis. This is an organization which, quarterly, supplies a list of story ideas and pictures.

The editor can, on request, receive a full-length feature story, complete with illustrations, on any subject listed in the quarterly issue. The only remuneration demanded is a tear sheet of the story and any pictures, if and when published. The big drawback is that there always is a commercial message, because each feature is written by the public relations department of some organization.

The editor should use these features mainly to get ideas for writing his own features, tailored to his organization. Occasionally, when the subject is universal, a feature can be adapted with very little change.

Ideas are the yarn with which the editor weaves his publication. So, the editor should be willing to accept ideas from every and any source available. Without ideas, an editor is lost. The stories are not going to walk in and write themselves. The company publication editor has to be a digger, dreamer, and doer, a versatile, nosy reporter, and a fussy, conscientious editor.

VARIATIONS ON THE SAME THEME

Music lovers are familiar with the classical song, "Bolero," written many years ago by Maurice Ravel. "Bolero" consists entirely of dozens of variations on the same musical theme. Each slightly different variation follows in turn after the other at a slightly greater volume, until the composition ends in a crashing crescendo.

In many ways, a company publication resembles an orchestration of dozens of Boleros or continuing themes. The main difference is that the publication never reaches the final crescendo. Instead, the house journal continues to play more and more slightly different variations from the same basic themes, over and over and over again, probably to infinity.

Though each company's publication may have themes which vary somewhat from the publications of other companies, they are similar from company to company. The simple fact is that each company faces about the same problems faced by each and every other company. The more closely alike the companies are in form, the more closely alike are their problems.

Many of the same problems which plague a company this week are going to be waiting to be solved next week, and the next and the

147

next and the next, through whole generations of editors, supervisors, managers, clerks, and production people.

Because of this, the editor is going to have to treat the same problems many times, with variations, in one year, and continue to write stories, articles, and editorials, take pictures, run cartoons, cajole, plead, and persuade on those same themes throughout his productive life.

Sometimes the treatment will be in the form of a news story; for example, a story that the organization has been cited for its contributions to safety by the National Safety Council. Next, there might be an "inquiring reporter" feature asking the question, "How Can I Promote Safety on the Job?"

Another month, the editor might try his hand at an editorial pointing out the dangers of inattention on the job. There might be a "telling" feature on blindness showing employees wearing blindfolds and trying to perform such simple things as lighting a cigaret, shaving, eating soup, etc.

Another good approach is an interview of management concerning one of the themes which the editor must feature. Although it is always a good idea to feature the production employees a high percentage of the time, it also is a good idea to feature management with some frequency. Although employees further down the ladder may give the impression at times that they do not trust or believe management, they still put a great deal of credence in what management says.

It is wise in presenting such an interview to be sure that management discusses subjects pertaining to the organization and answers questions which are uppermost in the minds of the employees. It is easy for this type of feature to degenerate into rather patent pats on the back by management for doing its job, or a weak rehash of company accomplishments during the past year.

In order to be effective, this type feature must deal frankly with the pertinent questions which are on the minds of employees. There should be no shying away from a long list of taboo areas, or the employees will soon recognize the feature as phony; it is better not to write it.

Some top examples of forthright frankness in discussion of issues were stories appearing in the rubber companies' publications in late 1971, concerning the reasons that production jobs were leaving Akron, Ohio. In those features, management met the issue head-on. The results were honest, two-way cooperation between company and union in attempts to make the Akron tire building plants competitive with American factories outside Akron and with foreign tire factories.

A telling adjunct to sharp writing is art work which can tell the story graphically and in little space. A skilled artist can simplify a complex problem, although one must beware of putting 100 percent reliance on simplistic solutions to problems for which there are no simple solutions.

If there is enough money in the budget, it can be extremely

effective to hire a professional cartoonist to prepare some art concerning a specific problem.

Sometimes very good artists can be hired at a surprisingly economical cost to prepare material for the editor. This is especially so if the artist is a full-time employee of a newspaper or magazine and wants to do some occasional free-lance work.

In this case, the editor can discuss with the artist the concept with which he is to deal. Sometimes the editor may have a firm idea of what the cartoon should be about and can visualize it, but lacks the ability to draw. In this case, the editor should feed his ideas to the artist and then see if the artist can translate these ideas onto paper.

In almost any large organization, there is sure to be one or more persons who draw or paint for a hobby. The editor should be able to judge whether the employee is competent enough to produce material of professional standards. If this is the case, the editor quite likely can use some of the employee's work, provided the employee is willing to produce art which fits the editor's needs.

Quite likely the editor will find that the employee wants no more remuneration than the satisfaction of seeing his work in print. On the other hand, the editor may find it necessary to pay the employee a small fee as incentive to get him to produce the desired art.

In any circumstance, the editor should have the employee sign a release. This will give the company all rights to the art work. In this case, the payment of $1.00 is legally binding. The editor should get the help of the company's legal counsel in preparing such a release form.

Fillers present another opportunity to sell the company's message(s) to the audience. Newspapers and magazines use one- or two-sentence fillers to achieve balance in makeup. Newspapers, in particular, use small items to fill space at the bottom of a column when there is not enough room to run a regular story. Any editor worth his salt can prepare a supply of fillers pertaining to the organization and have them ready to fit into small blank spaces on the pages; or a subordinate staff member can be assigned to do this job.

The editor should realize that fillers are very well read, so there should be considerable thought to their preparation. Reader's Digest is one example of a magazine which makes telling use of very short items at the bottoms of pages. Quite probably the short items are better read than the three- or four-page features.

A valuable device of most publications is the change-of-pace item or feature which is used to balance the regular fare. The Wall Street Journal is a telling case in point. On the Journal's front page, amidst the heavy daily dosage of business news, there usually are two or three columns devoted to well-researched features, sharply written by writers who handle their subjects with intelligence, wit, and good taste.

The industrial editor would do well to adapt the same scheme to his publication(s) and present the lighter side of the business by means of these change-of-pace features.

Such articles can do double duty by playing up employees' interests. An article might feature an employee's unusual hobby, the athletic prowess of a son or daughter, an unusual vacation, or a housewife's recipe. Stories might also be included that show appreciation for the employees. The list is almost endless and can be restricted only by the outer limits of the editor's imagination.

The editor should keep in mind, however, that features should not take over the publication. There should be enough features to lighten the look of the book and entice the readers to read. Otherwise, the editor is not doing his job for the organization. The editor should never forget that it is his job to promote the organization. He is a salesman as surely as if he were promoting the product in a company store.

It might be well at this point to inject a word of caution to the editor who sees the feature approach as a chance to slough off the job. All features should be staff-written about the organization, and all pictures used should concern the organization.

For example, a feature about organic farming, picturing a pretty 4-H girl, would not fill the bill. Such a feature can be company-slanted if the editor can find a company employee who is engaged in organic farming and can feature that employee. Of course, it would be entirely appropriate to take a picture of the employee and his pretty daughter to illustrate the item.

By the same token, the editor should be on the lookout to see if there can be a tie-in of the company's product. For example, while at Firestone, the author was able to feature the durability of Firestone tires in several instances when employees took extended vacations by automobile. In one case, an employee drove to Alaska and back without serious tire trouble.

Because of the popularity of "action line" types of columns in daily newspapers and the tremendous pull of the "letter to the editor" in dailies, some company publication editors think they should use similar features.

There is no definitive answer to whether or not the editor should carry a gripe or complaint column.

Some organizations apparently feel that such a column is highly successful; other organizations sincerely doubt its value.

One of the reasons such a column might be needed is the slowness of moving information from the employee up the line to management. Sometimes the channels of communication are almost totally blocked between employee and management. Occasionally, channels seem purposely plugged. In these cases, the "action line" or "letter" column might be the means needed to inform management of situations of which it might not be aware. There might be a middle manager somewhere who is blocking communication as a means of covering up incompetence, etc.

On the other hand, some organizations feel that the reporting procedures from employee to management are efficient and the formal channels of communication are open and effective. In these instances, management will feel that a "letter to the editor" or "action line" column is merely giving chronic malcontents and troublemakers a chance to air their personal gripes against the company, supervisors, or personal enemies.

In almost every large organization, there is a union with which the company has established grievance procedures. If the union member has a grievance, the grievance is handled in a regularly prescribed manner through the shop steward.

Usually the company will have a suggestion system by which the employees can make suggestions for the changing of work standards, installation of safety devices, or other changes in the mode of company operations.

Most companies also have safety directors and committees to which employees can report dangerous equipment or procedures.

When a company has these procedures and others for handling employee complaints or grievances, there is some justice to the feeling that a "gripe column" in the company publication serves no useful purpose.

In the final analysis, the policy of the company, plus the mature judgment of the editor, would decide whether an "action line" type of column is needed.

The International Association of Business Communicators has a voluminous reference file in the office in San Francisco. This contains top stories on almost any conceivable subject, such as safety, suggestions, waste, etc. The association issues, from time to time, brochures of aids for industrial editors. This office offers a gold mine of materials and services to help both the beginning and the established industrial editors. Files of stories on given subjects can be borrowed from the office so an editor can study the handling of these stories by top editors.

By all means, if the editor's organization is unionized, he should be sure to exchange with the international publication of the union which represents his company's employees. It makes sense to see what the union is saying about one's company. This publication should be read to furnish background information. The company's labor relations executives are reading the publication, and so should the editor.

If his union local publishes a sheet, he should ask to be put on that mailing list too. It is a mistake for the editor to live in sublime ignorance of the union's printed message to his audience.

For a general background briefing on business, the editor should subscribe to, and read daily, The Wall Street Journal. The Journal is the nation's best daily wrap-up of business news. Not only that, the Journal has some of the best feature writing to be found.

If an editor is having some problems with his writing style, he should study the Journal and try to emulate the successful formula used by its staff members. Journal personality sketches make the subjects come alive.

Another suggestion is to subscribe to and read the weekly National Observer. The Observer, even more than the Journal, is the master of the in-depth feature, the roundup story dealing with a complex issue. What makes the Observer writing so telling is that the editors apparently are not writing from a predetermined viewpoint.

Of course, the editor should subscribe to, and read the daily paper(s) in the city in which the organization is located.

If possible, he should subscribe to the top trade journals which serve the business in which his organization is engaged. If his organization is engaged in rubber production, sales, etc., the editor should subscribe to the trade journals which deal with rubber, such as Rubber World. Of course, the publication may not allow him to become a subscriber. In this case, he should find out which executive in his organization subscribes and arrange to borrow his copy each month.

The editor can get the names of trade journals or business papers from one of several services--Business Publication rates and data, Bacon's Publicity Checker, or Gebbie's All-in-One Directory.

In addition to these publications, the editor should do occasional reading and/or skimming through such publications as Saturday Review, New Yorker, Harper's, etc., and a variety of other magazines. By reading a wide range of publications, the editor can see what is new in writing styles, makeup, and layout. Some of these graphic innovations might possibly be adapted profitably by the editor in his publication.

He should keep one thought foremost in his mind. . . . When a creative person stops learning, he is done.

Chapter

16

PICTURES THAT TELL STORIES

"One picture is worth more than ten thousand words"--Chinese proverb.

A picture has the ability to convey at a glance the meaning which would take columns of text to explain.

Words can say a man looks tired; a picture can show just how tired. Words can say a woman is beautiful; a picture can show just how beautiful. Words can say the Grand Canyon is big; a picture can show the awesome majesty of the enormous cleft.

The picture conveys the idea easily, so the reader does not have to work. Words force many minutes or hours of painstaking work on the part of the reader to extract the meaning and nuances.

The meaning conveyed by a picture is universal; each word may take on a slightly different connotation for each reader. For example, a picture of a shapely nude woman carries a universal message to a Russian, an American, a Frenchman, or anyone else. However, the word "democracy" might convey one meaning to a Russian, a second meaning to an American, and a third meaning to a Frenchman, etc.

Most persons prefer to gain the majority of their information using a pictorial or graphic approach. This answers part of the reasons why television has been slowly killing the nation's general circulation magazines.

The lesson for the industrial editor is: to communicate successfully, it is necessary to make use of pictures.

The first question is--what kind of pictures? The answer: pictures which apply to the organization; pictures which are in focus; pictures which are of good quality; pictures which tell stories simply and quickly.

Before the publication is started, there must be a decision as to the sources of pictures--who is going to take the pictures, who is going to process them once taken, and who is going to make the decision of which pictures to use.

The new editor may have a job convincing his organization that very few persons combine the talents of top-level photographer with top-level writer. Writers think words; photographers think pictures

The editor is going to be busy handling the various aspects of interviewing, editing, writing copy and headlines, gaining clearances, and handling production and layout, so that he is not going to have time to add the duties of taking pictures, developing negatives, making prints, ordering film, doing maintenance on the cameras and the other myriad duties connected with photography.

It is true that on many monthly company publications the editor handles all of the photographic chores in addition to his editing duties. There are some advantages to this procedure, if the publication is small and the auxiliary duties of the editor are limited

In these cases, the editor knows exactly what he wants in the way of a picture to illustrate a given feature. He can set up the photographic assignment exactly as he envisions, without having to spend time briefing someone else on the story line and how the picture should be handled.

However, an editor with a smaller publication oftentimes has public relations duties to perform in addition to his editor-photographer chores. This same editor might have photography assignments not connected with the publication.

There is the possibility that the editor, as public relations man, might be asked by the organization to be at a meeting downtown; and, at the same time, he might be needed as photographer of a production process or of some new construction.

The editor, as photographer, might also face a situation in which the organization wants him to rush through the production of a couple hundred prints in the darkroom; and, at the same time, he is scheduled to do the final reading of page proofs at the printer's.

If the company wants a top-quality publication, the editor should be freed from the additional duties of photography. In this case, there are several alternative routes for securing pictures.

If the company is willing and can afford it, probably it is best if there is a top-notch photographer hired for the specific purpose of taking publication pictures. Such a photographer should be one whose training has fitted him for news photography and not portrait work.

In a pinch, of course, a studio or portrait photographer can be trained to do a competent job of publication photography; but it is better if the photographer has training in news pictures.

Although the publication photographer's main duties will be to take pictures for the publication(s), he could in his spare time take pictures for a news bureau, personnel, engineers, or other departments. The editor should make sure procedures are set up whereby no work is done without a work order. Then the photographer should keep track of all time spent on outside assignments and of all pictures and materials used, and the appropriate departments would be charged back accordingly. Otherwise, the publication would find itself rapidly losing control of its photographer.

If the organization already has a photography department, the publication might be in the situation of having to institute work orders to get publication pictures.

If the organization does not have a photography department and cannot or will not hire a full-time publication photographer, possibly the editor can secure the services of a free lance. The editor should have a clear understanding of the rate to be charged and a written contract with the free lance. It should always be stipulated that negatives are the property of the editor. He should keep control of all negatives and pictures taken, with the negatives kept on file in his office and not in the office of the free lance.

In trying to sell the organization on the desirability of having a full-time publication photographer, the editor should emphasize that the company can exercise better control over photographs if the photographer is a full-time employee.

The publication photographer will be valuable to the organization not only in taking pictures for the publication, but in auxiliary photographic roles. In fact, with very little additional training, a good still photographer can learn to produce motion pictures to use as training films.

However the photography is handled, the editor should make sure each picture used is top quality and makes a meaningful contribution to the publication. Good pictures, judiciously used, can add sparkle to a well-written publication. Poor-quality pictures are worse than useless; they will spoil what might otherwise be a top-quality effort.

As to the method of planning pictures for an industrial publication there are two basic schools of thought.

Some photographers, who prefer to be known as "photojournalists," usually go by the credo that a picture should never be posed. Some of these photojournalists spend a day or more exposing several rolls of film in order to produce one or two usable pictures.

The author appreciates the dedication and honesty of the photojournalist. Industrial editors will do well to study the methods of the photojournalists and take to heart their methods of operation. The photojournalists are constantly trying to get realism into their pictures. They always strive to get their photographs to tell a story.

On the other end of the scale is the photographic "routineer." This individual always sets up a picture. Quite often the "routineer" will use one formalized pose for all pictures which deal with the same situation. For instance, the "routineer" might always use basically head-and-shoulder pictures. The author has seen company publications with 50 or more head-and-shoulder pictures of employees who had observed anniversaries with the company. Such publications resemble nothing quite so much as high school annuals.

Other "routineers" will almost always have every picture consist of persons shoved into a corner or against a wall, tell them to say "cheese," and then expose some film.

For the industrial editor, there needs to be a midpoint, somewhere between the photojournalist and "routineer." Although the editor may not necessarily take the pictures, he should have sufficient knowledge to be aware of the problems involved in securing good pictures and to judge quickly whether a picture is good or bad.

The editor should bring the photographer in for a long briefing concerning the whole focus of a given issue while the publication is being planned. As each point is discussed, the editor and the photographer should both advance ideas on the best way to handle the photographic aspects. Except in rare instances, photographs for publication should not be spur-of-the-moment.

This means the editor and the photographer should avoid the all-too-frequent procedure of a company executive's calling the office with a report that, "John Employee is going to get a suggestion award in five minutes. Come and get a picture for the publication."

The whole organization should be thoroughly briefed on the importance of planning ahead for the publication. In the above situation, it is suggested that the resultant picture be used on the bulletin board or presented to the recipient.

For the publication, it would be best for the recipient to be pictured in some pose related to the suggestion which brought the award.

This method will make the editor and the photographer work harder. It is not easy to come up with good, meaningful, story-telling pictures for every situation.

The planning for the publication will be slow and painstaking, with an issue planned as much as six months ahead. Sometimes the issue might be drafted roughly, page by page, even before the interviewing is done. However, care should be taken to avoid being too rigid. The editor should be flexible enough that, when an exceptionally good feature appears, he can give it more space than originally scheduled.

Through such planning sessions, the editor and the photographer will come up with several good ideas for poses to illustrate each specific feature.

The editor may want to convey to the reader the amount of raw material wasted daily in production processes. With the photographer, he might decide to picture a pile of waste material heaped on the front lawn of the plant.

For the industrial publication, most pictures and stories must be contrived. The production of a picture must be planned to the last detail.

With all due regard to the photojournalistic technique of waiting around for hours or days to get the right picture, the industrial or business situation does not lend itself to such leisurely treatment.

In the first place, a picture must say exactly what the editor wants it to say. Therefore, most pictures must be posed. For a production situation, there must be provision for a specific time at which the pictures will be taken. The disruptive process of picture taking must be limited to a specific length of time so the curtailment of production can be held to a minimum.

The editor and the photographer must take specific steps of clearance with certain company persons before the pictures can be taken.

For example, the idea of a picture must be cleared with the editor's boss. If the idea is approved, it must be cleared with the head of the department who supervises the specific production process. This means the department head must know exactly when the pictures will be taken and the approximate amount of time needed to take them.

Because the publication wants to present the organization in a good light, the area should be clean. Sometimes it is desirable to have certain machines painted before pictures are taken.

The editor should be sure the production person who will appear in a picture is willing to pose. The editor should make certain the individual is reasonably presentable. These two facts having been decided, the editor and/or the photographer should obtain a written clearance from the employee.

Because of the wide variance of attire worn by production persons, it will sometimes be better to have on hand a stock of company shirts or long coats which the employee can wear. This step would insure a standard appearance in those cases where the employee's working attire happens to be unattractive.

The photographer should be trained to make certain that the picture-taking area is clean and presentable, because these pictures are for publication; therefore, it will reflect upon the organization. If it happens that the area as pictured is untidy, the manager is going to have to answer to management on the subject of sloppy housekeeping. If this happens, that manager will be less willing to allow future picture taking in his area. For this reason, it is a good idea to have the area's supervisor or manager on hand for the picture taking. If possible, a Polaroid picture should be taken first, and the supervisor should be allowed to examine it before the photographer makes the publication photograph.

After the picture is enlarged, a copy should be shown to the supervisor to see if it meets with his approval. A copy should be sent through clearance channels to make doubly sure company secrets will not be revealed.

For other pictures, in which production equipment and processes are not being depicted, there is less need for this great amount of caution. However, the pre-planning for these pictures is just as necessary.

It is best if the editor and the photographer plan in minute detail all steps of carrying out each assignment. It is well if a sort of shooting script be prepared. The persons who will appear in the picture should be chosen with care to make sure they reflect the impression the editor seeks to convey.

In choosing models, the editor should strive to feature typical employees rather than using management and white-collar employees. This is especially so if the organization has a high percentage of production employees.

Some company publications with lazy editors will almost invariably depend upon white-collar employees for models. What is worse, one multi-national organization quite frequently has used employees from the publication department to illustrate its features. Several times, this organization has used children of the photographers and public relations executives to illustrate features.

Editors and photographers who do this need someone to prod them out of their lethargy and urge them to seek their models from among the ranks of production employees. Otherwise, the readers will react adversely.

The editor and the photographer should always keep alert for the picture of opportunity, the picture which occurs outside the planned format, or the picture which involves a disaster. Naturally, the editor is going to hope no disasters occur.

However, there are going to be minor mishaps or fortuitous occurrences which are going to present themselves as picture possibilities. One example might be if a heavy piece of equipment falls on an employee's foot. If the employee was wearing safety shoes, a picture can be taken--and used--pointing up the fact the employee's toes were saved because he was wearing safety shoes.

If there is an explosion or fire, a picture can be used; then an accompanying story or cutlines can point up the need for more care, to avoid loss of lives, injuries, lost production, or loss of jobs.

One of the big problems faced by editors is the unsolicited picture. If the publication has no policy on this, a policy should be established quickly. Unsolicited pictures should be used only if they fit in with the theme of the publication--and then only if the pictures are of the same professional quality produced by the staff or suppliers.

Polaroid snapshots of an employee's Aunt Minnie, standing on the edge of the Grand Canyon, usually do not lend themselves to use in any company publication. On the other hand, if the picture is of good quality and fits in with the theme of the publication, use it.

For instance, if Aunt Minnie is camping on the rim of the Grand Canyon and the camping equipment is made by the editor's company, that picture would be a natural for the publication.

The editor's organization might be one of many which sponsors an employee vacation photo contest. If so, the contest should be publicized far in advance so the employees can have time to plan some good pictures. Then, some qualified judges who are not con-nected with the company should be chosen to pick the winners. In this case, it is a good idea to run the winning submissions as well as the better "also ran" pictures. The purpose of such a contest is employee recognition; it also points out to the readers that employees range pretty far afield on their vacations--therefore, the employees must be well paid if they can afford to take such extensive vacations.

Chapter

17

CHOOSING AND WORKING WITH SUPPLIERS

"It ain't what you do, it's the way what you do it," goes a song of the 1930s.

That phrase is particularly appropriate to the company editor working inside corporate guidelines, especially in choosing and working with suppliers.

For most corporate editors, printing will represent a purchased service. That is, the editor's company will not print the publication. The printing will have to be contracted to a job shop. In some cases, the distribution also will be handled by an outside supplier.

Actually the editor who has to purchase printing outside of his organization probably has a happier working situation than if he has to use an in-house printer.

With an outside printer, the editor authorizes payment of the printing bill, so the printer will work harder to please him. An in-house print shop owes greater allegiance to company officials higher in the corporate structure. This means the publication does not have top priority. In a pinch, the publication is going to take a back seat in favor of higher priority work.

An editor who has a choice would be well advised to choose an outside supplier, unless, of course, the job can be done more economically at home. The IABC _News_ has pointed out that a growing number of company publications are being printed in-house by offset or electrostatic printing systems. In the constant battle to hold the cost line, it behooves the communicator to keep constantly in touch with the services available in his own company. If a satisfactory job can be performed in-house more economically than it can be purchased, it is only good common sense to produce the work at home.

The first step in choosing a supplier is to ask the immediate superior the customary company procedure involving purchases. Usually all purchases are funneled through a purchasing agent or department. The name may vary, and there may be slight differences in procedures, but the principle is fairly standard from business to business.

The editor should discuss his needs with the purchasing department and seek advice concerning how to choose suppliers. The purchasing agent may suggest the editor contact suppliers on his own or offer to contact potential suppliers for him. In any case, the editor should supply specific information concerning the services or supplies wanted.

In choosing a printer, the editor should be specific on frequency of publication, number of pages, page size, format, and quantity of copies per issue.

The editor should specify the printing style. Since letter-press is a rapidly fading style, probably the job will be done off-set.

Because offset is more sophisticated, there are some aspects of which the editor should be aware. One of these is the phrase "camera ready." This means all composition and paste-up must be done before the job is taken to the printer. If the editor's organization can't produce composition, a second supplier will have to set the type.

Almost all makeready, which in letterpress is done by the printer, in offset is done by the editor or editor's agent. With letterpress, the editor makes a rough dummy and the printers put all of the type neatly into forms. With offset, the editor or his agent(s) must produce a final paste-up in which everything is pasted down neatly. The offset printer takes a picture of this paste-up, and in effect, the printing is done from that picture.

This means that if a line is pasted a little crooked, that is the way the printed job will be--a little crooked. If the person doing the paste-up spills a drop of coffee on it, the drop of coffee will appear in the final job. The same thing applies to smudges, fingerprints, fly specks, cigar ashes, and excess glue.

It is best for the offset editor to hire an artist to do the final paste-up.

Offset is probably not cheaper than letterpress; it may be just that the offset shop provides fewer services and therefore charges a correspondingly lower fee.

In choosing the print shop, the editor should find out exactly what kinds of type faces are available for body and headline type. For a tabloid newspaper, the shop should be able to offer a headline schedule which runs from about 14 point through at least 36 point, in one type family, both Roman and Italic. Some shops will not have such a collection, but instead have a hodgepodge of headline type--14 point in one family, 18 point in a second, 24 point in a third, etc. The editor should steer clear of such a shop unless he just plain doesn't care what his publication looks like. Such a shop is almost certain to be sloppy and slipshod in its work, and very lax in meeting deadlines.

Before giving a contract to a print shop, the editor should be sure the owner can show him the body type available. Body type comes in several type families, as does headline type. Some type families look smaller for a given size than other families. For instance, an 8-point type in one style presents a smaller image than 8-point type in another style. This means the editor should be sure to compare the appearance of various body type faces before choosing the one for his publication. In the contract, the exact type face should be specified, as well as the point size.

The purchasing department is going to favor the supplier that will submit the lowest bid. This is natural because it is the department's job to help the company watch costs.

It is the editor's job to make sure the company receives quality printing, economically produced. This means he should make sure the supplier can do the job without extravagant frills. It also means he should be open and aboveboard in dealing with the purchasing department and all other departments.

During the search for a supplier, the editor should ask for work samples, if appropriate. He should also ask for names of current customers, talk to these customers in confidence, and try to ascertain their feelings about the supplier. The work area should be observed. If most employees seem happy, busy and neat, probably the shop is good. If work areas are cluttered, ill-lighted and dirty, and employees slow moving and surly, chances are the organization is having problems and will neither produce top quality, nor meet deadlines.

If the purchasing department recommends one supplier and the editor feels a second supplier can do a better job, the editor should explain to the purchasing agent specifically why he prefers number two to number one. Such choices should be based on reason rather than emotion, friendship, or nepotism. Above all, the overriding consideration will be "what is best for the company." Both editor and purchasing agent should be working toward this goal, as should all of the organization's employees.

A contract with a supplier should cover as many contingencies as possible. For example, does the printer have alternative means of producing a company's job if his equipment breaks down? What will be the extra charge for a second printing of the same material? What will be the extra charge if the print order is boosted? The purchasing department has years of experience in establishing specifications and will be glad to help set them up. The editor should ask one or more other editors for suggestions concerning contracts with suppliers. It never hurts to know a little more about a subject.

After the contract is signed, the editor and the supplier should immediately agree upon a schedule which will include deadlines. Sometimes such deadlines will be incorporated into a contract. Before the editor can establish deadlines, he must have a firm idea of how long it will take to accomplish each step of the operation. Again, it might be helpful for the editor to discuss deadlines with another editor, and then adapt the latter's to his situation. There should be plenty of leeway in the schedule to take care of contingencies. Other things should be kept in mind, such as holidays, illness, machine breakdowns, off days, etc. Even with plenty of time figured in for such contingencies, there will be times when the editor will forego sleep or will work through a weekend to meet a deadline.

He should be sure to keep every deadline--or better yet, be a little early. If the editor does not meet his deadline, this will indicate to the supplier he really is not serious about the schedule. The supplier then will not feel duty bound to keep his deadlines. If in spite of all best efforts, the editor cannot meet a deadline, he should call the supplier at the earliest opportunity and explain the reason. Also, he should tell the supplier approximately when the promised material will be ready.

A conscientious supplier will have a time slot allotted for the job. If the supplier knows ahead of time the job is delayed, another job can be scheduled into that time slot. Otherwise, personnel and equipment may be kept idle in anticipation of a job which does not arrive. The supplier's costs are the same whether the personnel and equipment are working or idle. The editor might have to pay these costs.

The best way to make sure a supplier keeps the deadlines is for the editor to keep the deadlines. It is a good idea for the editor to check from time to time with the supplier while the job is in progress. However, he shouldn't make a nuisance of himself. If the supplier is close enough and the editor has the time, he can drop in and offer to take the supplier to coffee. The supplier will get the point that the editor is vitally interested in this job. While they are drinking coffee, the editor can casually ask him how the job is going.

With printing, a checking copy should always be read before the full press run is made. Errors have a way of creeping into print, so one cannot be too careful in the attempt to avoid errors.

It is necessary to tell the printer what to do with the copies. Sometimes the printer will handle the distribution. In this case, the printer handles the addressing and sorting and takes the bundles to the post office.

If the distribution is to the employees at work, the method of delivery from the printer should be stipulated. No detail should be left to chance.

The guideline in working with suppliers is good communications. The editor should keep in constant touch with each supplier concerning the job in progress. He should be specific as to what is to be done. He should also make sure that he keeps his deadlines and the supplier keeps his deadlines. Above all, he should demand top quality. If the supplier is not able or willing to produce quality work, the editor should find a supplier that will.

The editor should be open and aboveboard with each supplier and make certain the supplier is open and aboveboard with him. The editor shouldn't ask personal favors or expect suppliers to handle his personal jobs and include the cost in the bill for company work. He should never agree or imply that there will be any under-the-table payments, bonus payments, or hidden charges on the bill. The job specification or contract should clearly spell out what is to be done and what the cost will be.

Some contracts will spell out a bonus arrangement for work done above and beyond the contract, or done earlier than the normal deadline. There also might be penalty clauses in the contract. However, any such bonuses or penalties should be clearly spelled out.

Chapter

18

PUTTING IT TOGETHER

The publication is the payoff. All the theory in the world is useless unless it is put into practice. The editor must be a self-starter who can discipline himself to do the actual work of gathering information, writing, clearing, editing, and marking for the printer all of the copy and art needed for the publication. Then, he must ride herd on the publication through each phase of production, including its distribution.

Editorial production takes up a significant part of the editor's time, even when the editor, typically, has a variety of other duties. The production aspects of editing are often almost totally ignored in books on editing and writing because authors assume that the editor knows the steps necessary to put the publication together. This book makes no such assumption. The author knows the editor may not have the faintest idea of how to go about getting a piece of copy in shape for the printer, or a picture ready for the engraver.

Assuming that the editor is just starting out in the house journal field and never has gone through the motions of producing a printed piece, he should follow these directions, some of which have been covered in earlier chapters:

1.   Keep Everything in a File

Take a file folder and label it with the name of the publication, the month or week, the volume number, and the issue number. If it is the first issue, it will be volume one, number one. The volume number changes on the anniversary date of the first issue. Keep everything pertaining to one issue in the same folder. Make at least one carbon copy of everything produced for the issue. Keep this file folder and all materials pertaining to the preparation of this issue on file for at least five years—longer, if your company will permit. You or a successor may want to reproduce the art 20 or more years from now, either in the same publication or in a company book. You are writing history. It is worth saving. Possibly no one else is keeping any coherent record of company events.

2.   Make a Story List

In your visits with various company officials, and through study of other company publications, make a list of proposed stories for your first issue. It is always better to have a list which is too long rather than too short. A good rule of thumb is about five proposed stories per page of a tabloid newspaper. Probably you should have about two proposed stories per page for a magazine. You should plan for variety in length of stories—some long, some short, and some medium. Have stories of general company interest, and others of lighter vein; maybe use an editorial; and write everything

178

non-timely. Make sure that you indicate the possibilities of pictures with several of the medium or long stories. Sometimes you might use a picture with no accompanying story. (See example of story list at end of chapter.)

Type your list of proposed stories, making at least one carbon. Take the original to your boss. Ask him to study the list for a day or two and indicate any additions or deletions. Be sure to keep the carbon in the special file you have started for the current month's publication. Be sure to keep at least one carbon of everything you write. Copy does get lost.

3.   Write the Stories

If a couple days go by and your boss does not return the proposed story list, ask him about it. Keep reminding him of the list and the need to get started to meet the deadlines. Keep up the gentle reminders until he approves the list.

When you have the list back, start immediately to interview people for stories, or in other ways to gather information from which to write. Take the necessary pictures to illustrate the stories, or have these pictures taken by a company photographer or a free lance.

Large companies often have professional artists on the payroll. If so, use them. Barring this, you may discover one or more of the employees whose hobby is art. Sometimes a spare-time artist will agree to draw illustrations without pay, other than the satisfaction of seeing his work in print. By all means put such a person to work. Cartoons drawn by a fellow employee take on added meaning for the reader.

Write each story in a rough form (don't forget a carbon), and submit a copy to the person you interviewed. This gives the individual a chance to correct any misstatements he might have made, or add points which he might have forgotten during the interview. Persons rarely realize the full impact of what they are saying until they see the material in writing.

When you have the subject's approval on his story, type it neatly on bond paper, and submit it through clearance channels which have been set up.

Management should understand that all corrections of stories must come at this stage of production and not when material has been set into type or when the final proofs are presented. Changes made on galley or page proofs are expensive, and management should realize this.

Management may prefer to clear all copy in one chunk. However, if your publication is sizable, this could be such a time-consuming job that a production jam would result. Probably it is better to have an agreement on what types of stories to clear, and clear them as written. Many stories probably will be of a non-sensitive nature, so they need not be cleared, except by your immediate superior. However, when in doubt, present the story for clearance.

Be sure that you also clear the pictures which go with the stories. Many times a picture can be more damaging than copy, because pictures get closer scrutiny. Organizations want to be shown in the most favorable light possible. A picture in which a production area tends to look messy, or in which there are obvious fire hazards, etc., would not depict the organization in the best light. Such a picture could lead to an unwanted inspection by safety or fire officials and result in higher insurance rates. Worse, you or the photographer might unwittingly picture an experimental process, thereby giving away company secrets through the publication. Clear those pictures.

You can help the company by submitting pictures of dirty or hazardous areas to management for action.

4.   Mark the Copy and Art

Each piece of copy, each piece of art must be identified by name of publication or organization. This is because you probably will have your printing done at a job shop. Job shops handle many jobs simultaneously. Unmarked copy gets lost easily.

Each piece of copy should be marked to tell the printer exactly what you want him to do with it. (See sample sheet of copy marked for printer, at end of chapter.) The printer wants to know the size and "family" of type and how many picas wide you want each line. He also wants to know the same information about the headlines.

It is probably best if your headlines are typed on sheets separate from those on which stories are written. For convenience, you can type all of the headlines of one size and family on one sheet; for example, all the 36-point Bodoni bold on one sheet, all the 30-

point Bodoni bold on another, etc. This procedure will make it easier for the shop and make the shop more helpful. If you help them, they'll help you.

Most of your art will consist of 8 x 10 glossy photographs. Make sure you identify each piece of art with the name of your publication or organization. Crop each piece of art to show the area you want engraved. (Cropped 8 x 10 glossy is shown at end of chapter.) Cropping is best done with a grease pencil, although a pen will do. You can do a better job of cropping if you use two L-shaped devices. These can be made by cutting them out of a large piece of cardboard. Use these devices to frame the area you desire to use in your picture. (See end of chapter for illustration of use.) Make the crop marks on the outer edge of the picture, and be sure the marks do not appear in the area to be engraved.

Print the instructions to the engraver on the back of the picture, outside of the area to be engraved.

Scale the picture to the desired size by use of a simple proportion slide rule, or a scaling wheel. If the engraving is smaller than the original copy, you gain in sharpness; if you make the engraving larger than the original copy, you lose in sharpness.

Your engraver will use either a slide rule, a proportion wheel, or both. He can tell you where to buy one or the other, or may even give you one. He also can tell you how to use one or the other of the devices. Using a proportion scale, decide the height and depth of the engraving, and then mark this information on the back of the picture, outside the space to be engraved. Express the proportions in picas rather than inches. Indicate the line screen to be used to make the engraving. Consult with the engraver before you decide what screen to use. Finer papers take a finer screen. Also, the screen differs from letterpress to offset. Tell the engraver exactly the grade of paper on which you are going to print; then he can advise you as to what screen to use for engravings.

5.   Copyread and Edit the Material

Copyreading is best done in a slow, painstaking manner. You have to force yourself to look at every word, which is an unnatural way of reading. Put the point of your pencil down underneath each word in turn, and focus your vision and thoughts on that word for a fraction of a second. This is the way you have to copyread and edit. You normally skim through reading material and do not really see all of a word. Copyread every bit of writing which is to go into the publication. If possible, have one or two other persons copyread the material.

Editing should be done with a medium (number 2) lead pencil, not with a ball-point pen. Any changes in copy should be done between the lines and should be printed, not written longhand. Remember that someone else is going to have to set your material into type. Very few persons produce really readable longhand. Go on the assumption that the printer will not be able to read your longhand.

Read each piece of copy several times--once for misspelled words, once for punctuation, once for grammar, once for factual errors, once for organization, once for lucidity, etc.; the total is up to you. (Standard copyreading symbols are listed at end of chapter.)

6.   Write the Headlines

If you do not know how to write headlines, buy a book on headline writing, copyreading, and editing. Learn the unit count system. Each newspaper headline should have an action verb and be written present tense. Stories are written past tense, third person. Do not end a line of a headline with a preposition, article, or conjunction.

Magazine headlines sometimes are labels and do not need verbs.

The headline should be a capsule summary of the story. Usually, you should be able to write a newspaper headline from the first paragraph. The latest newspaper style is to write the headlines lower case, except for the first letter of the first word and the first letter of each proper noun. The trend is to limit headlines to two lines. One expert recommends no more than about 35 units in one line of a headline.

For newspapers, it is best to use one basic family of headline type throughout the publication, for example, Bodoni bold with Bodoni italic for contrast. It is better not to mix type families. It is best to use a serif body type because serif type is more readable than sans-serif type. An exception is Optima, a sans-serif type which is highly readable.

A general rule in newspapers is that the bigger the story, the bigger the headline, and the higher you put that story on the page.

Before you give a bid to a print shop, be sure you have a schedule showing what is available in body and headline type.

It would be a good idea to buy a book on typography to assist you in this area. Some good ones have been written by Edmund Arnold of Syracuse University.

7.   Log the Copy and Art

Before you start preparing your stories, it is a very good idea to prepare a copy log, then keep a running record of how much material you have prepared in comparison with the total space to be filled. (Sample log is shown at end of chapter.) First, measure the proposed publication to see how much total space in column inches there is to fill. Enter this figure at the top of one column in the log. As each piece of copy or art is completed and filed in your folder, subtract the number of column inches contained in that piece from the total amount of space left to fill. You now know at all times where you stand in terms of copy produced and space yet to fill. Don't forget to use this same procedure with the flag, masthead, and self-mailer. A column inch is one inch deep, one column wide. Most newspaper columns are about 12 picas, or 2 inches wide.

You can estimate copy length by having your printer set 10 or more lines of copy, using the desired type in the pica measure you want to use for a standard column. Measure the material to deter-

mine how many lines you will have in an average column inch. Count
the units of copy so that you will know how many units, including
spaces, you will have in an average line. Set your typewriter
stops accordingly. That is, if you have 30 units (letters and
spaces) per line of type, set your typewriter stops at 10 and 70.
Then, for each line of typewritten copy, you will have two lines
of copy when they are set into type. On this basis, if you have
eight lines of type in a column inch, you will know that four lines
of typewritten material will produce one column inch of material
when set into type.

8.   Take the Copy to the Printer

When you have produced all of the copy and art needed for an
issue of your publication, obtained clearances, and marked everything properly, take the whole file to the printer. It is best if
you work directly with a shop foreman or an assistant rather than
a salesman. However, you may be unable to do this. In fact, you
may have to mail everything to a shop many miles away, in which
case your instructions to the printer must be most clear. If you
personally take the material to the printer, go through your file
of material, piece by piece, while a shop representative looks on.
In this way, you and he can be doubly sure that each piece is marked
correctly and that he understands the markings. Before you leave,
ask the foreman when he expects to start work on your copy and when
you can expect galley proofs.

From time to time you should "be driving by" the shop, drop

in, and offer to take the foreman to coffee (he'll buy because you are a customer). During coffee, ask about progress on your job. Your continuing interest will increase the possibility that the shop will meet the deadlines.

9.   Take the Art to the Engraver

After you have taken all copy to the printer, take all art to the engraver. Sometimes your printer also will be your engraver. This possibility becomes almost a certainty if you print offset. Use the same procedure with the engraver as with the printer. Go through the entire file of art, piece by piece, with the shop representative, to make sure that each piece is identified and clearly marked with instructions which are understood by the engraving shop. Be sure the engraver knows specifically on what grade of paper you plan to print. Have a clear understanding as to when the engravings will be completed, where the proofs will go, where the engravings will go, and who will deliver.

As with the printer, so with the engraver; it is an advantage to have the production done near your office. If your engravings are produced at a distance, you may be forced to use poor engravings because, by the time the engravings arrive, your deadline is here and you don't have time to have them remade.

10.   Get the Proofs from the Engraver and the Printer

Of course, if you are printing offset, the two sets of proofs will come from the same source.

You always will get at least two sets of proofs of copy and

art. You may want three or more sets of galley proofs so you can have several persons read the proofs at the same time.

As soon as you get the engraving proofs (which will be accompanied by the original art) examine the proofs very closely to see if they are of acceptable quality. Mark those in which the quality is not acceptable, return them (with the original art), and have them redone. Check the size of the engravings to see that they are made as marked. If any are not the size you specified, have those made over. Everyone makes mistakes, so never accept material without checking for conformance to your standards.

Read the galley proofs word for word against the copy which you sent to the printer. Make sure all material has been set as you have indicated. Do not "improve grammar" or in other ways make changes on the galleys except to make the composition conform to your copy as marked. Changes at this stage are expensive. Any editing and copyreading is behind you and should have been done before the copy was set into type. Print all corrections in red. If other persons are reading sets of galley proofs for errors, gather all sets and incorporate all corrections onto one set. This is the set which you will return to the printer along with the dummy.

11.   Prepare a Dummy or Layout

Your galley proofs will be marked by name of publication and numbered consecutively. On one set of the galleys, mark several paragraphs of each story with the same number that appears at the top of the galley. Use red pencil or pen and mark in bold numbers.

(This step is sometimes eliminated in offset.) This will help the printer in putting the type into page forms. Cut up this set of galleys so that each story is separated from all other stories and the border trimmed away. Cut up one set of engraving proofs so that each picture is separated from all other pictures and the borders trimmed away. Place the pictures, stories, headlines, flag, masthead, and any other element to be used, on the dummy sheets in the exact spots in which you want them to appear. You can get layout sheets from the printer, or you can dummy on top of sheets torn from the previous issue of your publication, or you can make dummy sheets from plain white paper.

Newspaper makeup uses little white space; magazine makeup usually uses lots of white space. Column rules are virtually a thing of the past.

Horizontal makeup is preferable to vertical. Horizontal makeup uses more stories of two or more columns. Vertical makeup uses many long, one-column stories. (Examples of the two styles are shown at end of chapter.) You should constantly study the front pages of several major dailies to see how they handle makeup, then adapt their devices for your publication. Use the same adaptive principle with magazines, if that is your format. The former Look and Life, the National Geographic Magazine, and others are good ones to copy. You can get examples of top industrial publications from the headquarters of the International Association of Business Communicators (IABC). The address is Suite 469, 870 Market Street, San Francisco, California 94102.

Here are some thoughts concerning newspaper layout:

* Have pictures comprise about 20 percent of the publication.
* Identify each picture directly underneath the picture.
* Don't use cutlines or captions above or to the side of the picture.
* Don't carry copy above or alongside the headline for that copy.
* Avoid continuing a story from page one.
* Avoid putting unrelated pictures in adjacent columns.
* Avoid "tombstoning"--aligning headlines in adjacent columns.
* Stick to one basic width for one-column material.
* Don't use a magazine format until you have had some training. Hire an expert to lay out your first issues if you use a magazine format.

Each editor has his own method of layout, usually deferring the job of pasting things in place until everything is as he wants it. One method is to get thick sheets of cardboard, thumbtack the dummy sheets to the cardboard, then temporarily thumbtack each item in place during the layout process. Once each element is in its desired place, you can paste down all items. A faster method is to tape everything onto the dummy sheets with transparent tape, and then pull out the thumbtacks. This will complete what is known as a rough dummy.

If you are printing letterpress, the printer will use the rough dummy to guide him in putting the elements into page forms.

If you are printing offset, there will be a set of proofs on slick paper. These are known as "repro proofs." Someone will have to make a final paste-up using the repro proofs and carefully paste every element into position exactly as it is to appear in the publication. This is no job for an unskilled person. It is probably better if the printer does the final paste-up, or if you have an artist do it. The job is time-consuming and must be done with great care. An item pasted crooked on the final paste-up will appear crooked in the final job. Any spot or smudge will show up in the print job.

After the dummy is completed, take it to the printer along with the corrected galley proofs. If any engravings are to be remade, have the printer give you the unacceptable engravings; then throw them into a wastebasket in your office.

12.   Read the Page Proofs

After the dummy (or final paste-up) has been in the print shop a couple days, the printer will have final proofs for you. Letterpress shops call them "page proofs"; offset shops call them "brown proofs." These proofs represent the last chance for you to correct errors before the job is printed. It is a good idea to get at least two sets of these final proofs.

The first step is to give these proofs a thorough reading to catch any uncorrected errors. You will have the corrected galleys back from the printer to assist in locating uncorrected errors.

After all the errors have been corrected in red, present the proofs to a top executive for clearance. Of course, you should have reached an understanding previously with this top executive that changes are not to be made at this stage of the game. At least, changes should be kept to a minimum because they now are extremely costly. If at all possible, have the top executive agree that the cost of any changes on final proofs will be charged to his account rather than to your budget. This should guarantee an absolute minimum of changes.

If there absolutely must be a change, be prepared with non-timely filler material which you can substitute if material is to be removed.

In checking the final proofs, be sure that the date on page one is the same as the dates on the other pages and in the masthead. It can be extremely embarrassing to have some pages dated June and other pages dated May in the same issue.

Once the top executive has initialed the final proofs, return them to the printer and point out the errors to him. Ask the printer when he expects to have the finished job for you. Get from the printer at least one copy of the publication early in the press run and read it for errors. If you see that errors marked on page proofs are appearing uncorrected in this printed copy, have the printer stop the press and correct the errors. Keep following the job through each phase of production.

13.   Distribute the Copies

Once printed, the publication must be distributed. Make sure the copies move into the distribution system as soon as possible. Distribution can be handled by a professional mailer, by the printer, or by you or your assistants.

If a professional mailer is to handle your distribution, be sure you know when the copies are delivered to the mailer from the printer; and be sure you know when the copies go from the mailer to the postoffice.

If distribution involves mailing, you will have a third-class (bulk) mailing permit. Do not maintain money on deposit to your account at the post office. Instead, deposit only enough money to cover the mailing after you know the copies have arrived at the post office. The reason for this suggestion is that other departments in your organization might try to pirate your mailing money. Someone may try to mail material using your mailing permit number and postage money. Protect your budget.

If your company believes mailing is too expensive, then you must set up your own distribution system. In this case, the printer will deliver copies of the publication to you. Distribution may be done by leaving copies at the company gates or in the lobby, or by carrying copies to each supervisor for distribution to the employees he supervises.

You still will want to mail to retirees, school libraries, opinion leaders, other editors, heads of other companies, etc.

In-plant distribution is possible only for an employee publication. If the house journal goes to salesmen, dealers, customers, or any one of several other publics, the copies probably will have to be mailed.

You also may want to leave copies in the company's lobby or waiting room. It is a good idea to have 100 or more extra copies of each issue on hand in your office to fill requests for them.

14.   Analyze Your Work

Now that the issue is distributed, analyze what is in it to see if you have achieved balance--that is, if you have lived up to the guidelines. You can do this with a content analysis or by a less formal study. By all means, listen for feedback in the way of letters and conversations and by discussing things with other editors and with known experts. Enter your publication in local and international contests run by the IABC.

It is a good idea to make periodic formal studies of the publication by means of surveys. It is best if the surveying is done by a qualified researcher. Several months of preparation should take place before a survey is undertaken. If your company has a marketing department, you may be able to get some help from that department in doing a survey.

15.   Plan Ahead

While you are in the midst of producing the current issue, you should have firm plans already made for the next period's publication, whether weekly, monthly, quarterly, or other. Many editors like to plan at least three issues in advance. Some magazines plan as much as a year in advance. You are, of course, continually working on features which can be used almost anytime, updating biographies, planning for special issues, and looking ahead at the calendar for possible tie-ins with holidays, such as Christmas, New Year's etc.

office remodeling
NASA
Miller promotion
new boiler
radial-age girl visits
AU gift
ecology
service awards
retirees
minority opportunities
first vacationer
January vacations
Hostetler retires
February retirees
controlling waste
Santa Arbogast retires
trade secrets bill
letter from soldier
Junior Achievement
satisfied customer
suggesters
appointments
memoriam
items within
20-year club trips
Red Cross needs blood
Gallon Club names
security
company uses video tape
yearly forecast
new product
news briefs
new factory
editorial--people can be customers
promotions
profile
product display
company history
keeping an eye on the competition
product highlights
plant roundup
the international picture
keeping healthy
energy conservation

Fig. 31--Example of story list.

January Journal
suggesters
lead

8 pt Spartan bold, flush left, 11½ picas

Suggesters Earn $2,600

Akron suggesters earned $2,600 in cash during a period from Oct. 16 to Nov. 30 for their ideas submitted to the suggestion program.

Elmer Hyrnick, machinist, 3990, collected $210 for his reduction maintenance idea to back brackets with steel bushings for large hose in 40-E. Barbara Schwiger, senior secretary, 2003, received a check for $110 for her better method to change the figuration for the Marietta Plant Incentive and Excess Labor Cost Report.

Award winners of $50 or more were as follows: John R. Handley, 3990, safety and improved traffic, $70; Edgar Williams, 7420, quality improvement, $50; Raymond Drexler, 3990, improved equipment, $60; Christy Karaginia, 7515, improved equipment, $55; Charles Infantino, 6533, improved equipment, $50; and Armand DiMascio, 7028, better method, $55.

Fig. 32--Example of lead story

Fig. 33--Example of cropped picture. (Courtesy, Dr. Harold Van Winkle, Kent State University School of Journalism)

Fig. 34--Example of use of cropping L's.

Symbol	Example	Meaning
$\mathcal{d}$	He made his mark**s**	take out
$\subset$	He made his mar◠k	close up
⌐	He made his mark	bring to mark
tr	He (his made) mark	transpose
stet	He made ~~his~~ mark	let it stand
#	mark. ∧All other	make paragraph
☐	∧He made his mark	indent em-quad
wf	He made ͡his mark	wrong font letter
lc	He made his /Mark	lower-case letter
sm c	He made <u>his</u> mark	small capitals
caps	He made <u>his</u> mark	capitals
ital	He made <u>his</u> mark	put in italic
rom	He made <u>his</u> mark	put in roman if rest is in italic
bf	He made his mark	put in bold face
⊙	He made his mark∧	period
⌄	He made Johns mark	apostrophe
⌄ ⌄	He made his∧mark∧	quotation marks
=/	This is a trademark	hyphen
#	He made hismark	space
vvv	He⌵made⌵his ⌵mark	even spacing
✗	He (made his mark	broken letter
‖	‖He made his mark	align
∗	∧He made his mark	insert reference mark

Fig. 35

COPY LOG

Item	Col. inches	Accum.	To go	Date
			600	
flag	7	7	593	1-3-74
mast	9	16	584	1-3-74
mailer	9	25	575	1-3-74
security	19	44	556	1-3-74
new tire	13	57	543	1-3-74
forecast	26	83	517	1-4-74

Fig. 36--Example of copy log.

Five School Systems Are Taking Part in Inner City Social Studies Project

More than 5,000 pupils in northeast Ohio schools are getting a different view of society in their social studies classes this year as a result of a Federally sponsored project labeled "FICSS."

The letters stand for "Focus on Inner City Social Studies," and to date four instructional units have been prepared and distributed for use by the teachers.

The units are "Families in Our City," for the primary grades; "The Afro-American in U. S. History," for grades 5, 8, and 11; "Nigeria: An African Dilemma," for grades 6 and 10; and "Minority Power in America," for grades 9 and 12.

Schools involved in teaching these units, and taking part in the project, are in Akron, Canton, Mansfield, Youngstown, and the Youngstown Diocese.

In coming months, participants of FICSS will look forward the develop-

ment of a completely new social studies curriculum which will encompass the kindergarten through 12th grade. Once this curriculum has been identified, the project will then be geared toward the identification and/or development of instructional units which will fulfill this design.

The units developed for use in 1968 are, therefore, emergency stop-gap units only. They may be utilized in the new curriculum or may be discarded if they are found to be contrary to the new curriculum.

The new curriculum as envisioned will attempt to give greater visibility and better perspective to all aspects of urban society and will be more relevant and sensitive to the needs and desires of inner city pupils than the curricula previously in use.

Project FICSS is being financed with an initial 15-month grant of $355,000

under Title III of the Elementary and Secondary Education Act and is to run to May 1971. The three-year expenditure for the project is estimated at approximately $666,000.

Director of the project is Dr. Melvin Arnoff, Associate Professor of Elementary Education at KSU and a specialist in the social studies. Assistant director is Gary Deonise, a new member of the special administrative staff of the College of Education assigned to FICSS. Office for the project is in Room 121, Education Building.

The Youngstown City School System is the sponsoring agency for the project and Walter Pyle, Youngstown Board of Education, is the fiscal officer.

Primary aim of the project, which was designed by Dr. Arnoff, is "to improve the quality of both course content and instructional techniques in the kindergarten through twelfth grade

social studies curriculum in the schools of the inner city." Inner city as used in the project includes all the schools of the five cooperating school systems.

The project got under way formally in the summer with an eight-week workshop on the KSU campus, directed by Dr. Arnoff and Mr. Deonise. The workshop ra nfrom June 24 to August 16, with 31 representatives from the five cooperating schools in attendance. That number included one social studies supervisor and from four to six teachers from each district.

The group spent the first six weeks of hte workshop in a "sensitization program" — in study and discussion, in hearing lectures and seeing films on urban problems. Among speakers and consultants were black students at both high school and college level, parents of inner-city children, and militants

(Continued on page 2)

KSU Education News

THE COLLEGE OF EDUCATION • KENT STATE UNIVERSITY • KENT, OHIO

Volume 5   Spring 1968   Number 2

Enrollment In Education Numbers 10,419

Student enrollment on the KSU campus this fall is 20,115. Another 7,010 are enrolled in the nine KSU branches and academic centers, bringing the overall enrollment to 27,125.

Among students on the main campus, 7,294 are enrolled in the College of Education. In the branches and academic centers, education students number 3,125, bringing the total of 10,419.

Of the education students, 450 are doing student teaching this fall in schools throughout northeast Ohio—76 in early childhood education, 141 in the elementary grades, 215 in secondary schools, 5 in special education, and 13 in speech and hearing. The number who will have done their student teaching in this academic year, plus a few who do student teaching in the summer, will exceed 1,700, according to Dr. Robert T. Pfeiffer, Director of Student Teaching.

A total of 3,435 degrees was awarded by KSU in 1968. Of that number, 2,568 were bachelors', 835 were masters', and 82 were doctors' degrees.

Those figures bring the grand total of masters' degrees to 7,328 since the first was awarded in 1936, and the grand total of doctors' degrees to 92 since the first was awarded in 1964.

All departments of the University now offer programs of study leading to the master's degree and 11 offer programs leading to the doctor's degree.

About 10 per cent of the total KSU enrollment this fall is at the graduate level. The number of graduate students is 2,688, compared with 2,193 last fall. Among the graduate students, 433 are doctoral candidates, compared with 263 a year ago.

Graduate study in the College of Education is growing rapidly. In terms of credit hours, it is two and one-half times what it was five years ago. As of August 27, the number of students actively engaged in graduate study in the College of Education was 2,703, including 2,439 at the master's level, 147 at the sixth-year level, and 117 at the doctoral level. (This does not mean that all those were necessarily enrolled in courses at that particular time, or in hte present fall quarter; but rather

(Continued on page 2)

Dean Schindler Elected Chairman Of Ohio Council

Dr. Clayton M. Schindler, Dean of the College of Education, was appointed a member of the Ohio Council on Teacher Education in October for a three-year term and shortly thereafter elected chairman of the Council.

As a member of the Council, Dr. Schindler will serve as a representative of the Ohio College Association. His appointment to the Council was announced by Dr. Glenn L. Clayton, President of Ashland College and currently President of the Ohio College Association.

The Council was established 15 years ago with Dr. Robert White, now President of KSU, its first president, to serve as an advisory body to the State Department of Education on teacher education.

It continues to serve in that manner, with a membership which includes four representatives of the Ohio College Association, three representatives of the Ohio Education Association, and one representative each of the Ohio Association for Student Teaching, the Ohio Association of Classroom Teachers, the Ohio Association for Supervision and Curriculum Development, the Ohio Association of Secondary School Principals, the Ohio Department of Elementary School Principals, the Ohio Association of School Administrators, and the Ohio Association of Colleges for Teacher Education.

Beginning with the next issue, KSU Education News will have a new editor. He is Dr. William A. Rodgers, Associate Professor of Secondary Education and Director of the Bureau of Educational Studies and Services. His office is in Room 400, College of Education Building; his telephone number is 672-2177.

Dr. Harold Van Winkle, Professor of Journalism and a member of the Graduate Education Faculty, has been editor since this publication was started five years ago.

Miss Rebecca Hendrix of East Sparta was presented the Amos Heer Scholarship at the Educational Leadership Day banquet on November 15.

The award is presented annually to the outstanding senior in the College of Education, determined on the basis of scholarship, leadership, and promise as a teacher.

The scholarship was established in 1960 by the KSU chapter of Kappa Delta Pi, national education honor society, in honor of Dr. Heer, who founded the chapter.

Miss Hendrix, a graduate of Sandy Valley High School in Stark County, has an overall grade point average of 3.85 (out of a possible 4.00). She is a student senator; vice president of her residence hall; a member of Laurels, honor society for senior women; a member of Epsilon Nu Gamma, English honorary; and is enrolled in the Honors College.

Speaker at the banquet, which is a part of the annual activities of Kappa Delta Pi, was Dr. Paul W. Briggs, Superintendent of Cleveland Schools.

Among students at KSU this fall are 297 from 58 countries other than the United States.

Student Teaching In Cali Planned For This Winter

Two programs in which education students will spend a quarter abroad will go into effect this academic year, according to present plans.

In the winter quarter, a number of students — perhaps 20 — will do their student teaching in Colegio Bolivar, a bi-national school in Cali, Colombia, South America.

By early November, 12 KSU students had signed to go to Cali and a number of others had indicated that they were interested. Four students at Northwestern University also have signed to take part in the program; and some from other colleges and universities, primarily in this area, may join the group, according to Dr. Robert T. Pfeiffer, Director of Student Teaching, who is directing the program.

Myron E. Wirick, Assistant Professor of Elementary Education, will accompany the group and serve as student teaching supervisor.

Plans have been completed and have been approved by President Robert I. White for an exchange of students and faculty members with Trinity and All Saints' Colleges (TASC), Horsforth-near-Leeds, England, in the spring quarter.

"It is hoped that 25 students and one faculty member will be available for the exchange," Dean Clayton M. Schindler said recently. "An equal number plans to come to Kent from TASC.

"Some selected students from neighboring colleges and universities would be welcome to join the group going from Kent," he said.

David J. Bowers, Graduate Assistant in the Dean's office, is coordinating this exchange program for the College of Education.

Plans are underway for ten students and one professor from Kent State University to spend the spring quarter of 1970 at the University of Kent in

(Continued on page 2)

Fig. 37--Example of paste-up dummy.

202

Chapter

19

DISTRIBUTING THE PUBLICATION

Once the publication is produced it must be distributed. The method of distribution will depend, in part, upon the audience and, in part, upon management thinking.

A very popular method of distribution, and probably the most effective, is through the U.S. mails. Less effective but more economical methods are to distribute through inter-plant mail, at company gates, in lobbies.

Although mailing to the home is more expensive and involves added work, many companies feel it is well worth the extra cost and trouble.

The reason is that a copy entrusted to the mails is almost 100 percent certain to arrive at the intended destination. Copies distributed at company gates, in lobbies, or through the in-plant mail system may not reach the intended recipient. Even though the recipient may get a copy, it will not necessarily arrive at the home. The recipient may read the publication at work and discard it; or the publication may be left in the car or thrown out on the way home.

If the publication does not arrive at home, an important secondary audience never gets a change to see it. That secondary audience consists of the family of the intended recipient and, quite often, neighbors and relatives.

In some ways, the secondary audience is more important than the primary. This is especially so of the employee publication. Company employees have some conception of the organization and its goals through appearing at work daily. The families, friends, and neighbors, on the other hand, have no valid source of information about the organization.

Most employees, if they discuss work at all, usually will regale family and friends with the aberrations of the departmental comic or some other irrelevancy. On rare times when an employee does discuss the company, the family is likely to hear a one-sided tirade over alleged mistreatment or a similarly confused and confusing account concerning benefits, contract negotiations, etc.

There might even be some employees who prefer to keep the family in ignorance of company business. During the author's tenure as a company publication editor, several employees requested to have their names dropped from the mailing list because they did not want their families to learn too much about the company. Before the publication had been established, one employee had been able to keep his family in ignorance of wage scales; others kept their families in ignorance of such fringe benefits as suggestion awards, scholarship programs, etc.

Another benefit of mailing employee publications to the home is the constant purging of the mailing list. People are notoriously lax in telling their correspondents about address changes. If the company mails a publication periodically to all employees, this means the company learns of address changes much faster than if it waits for the employee to make notification. There are times when it is essential to be able to reach all employees at current addresses. Therefore, it is extremely valuable to know that your mailing addresses are current.

When a company does not mail the employee publication to the homes, it sometimes finds unforeseen side effects. For instance, if distribution is through the in-plant mail system, it is almost a foregone conclusion that employees are going to read the publication on company time. Worse, the employee will not bother to take it home for the spouse and family.

Some companies distribute outside the company gates. This move makes it harder for the employee to read the publication at work. Some employees have been known to leave the journal in the car until they return to the factory on the next shift, and then read the publication on company time.

Whether the company mails the publication to employees, it is forced to use the mails to reach other audiences. For example, a journal for salesmen usually must be mailed to the salesman's home or office. The publication edited for stockholders must be mailed to the stockholder. Externals which may go to customers must be mailed to the customers.

But whether or not distribution is by mail or other means, the organization should not limit circulation to the primary audience. It is a good idea to have a supply of the current publication on hand in various company lobbies so they can be read and taken by visitors.

Provision should be made to give copies to persons who visit the company on formal tours.

Other distribution can be arranged to public and school libraries. Another potential audience is the opinion leaders. The extent to which these audiences are cultivated depends upon the scope of the organization's operations and the area over which it wants to extend its influence.

An organization which operates basically in one city might confine its opinion leader list to that city. A company which operates nationwide might feel motivated to develop opinion leader lists for all major cities.

In compiling an opinion leader list, the editor will choose the names of educators, manufacturers, entrepreneurs, businessmen, librarians, ministers, etc. Other categories usually included are customers and suppliers, presidents and/or secretaries of clubs, groups and organizations such as YMCA, FFA, women's clubs, and others.

Copies of the publication should go to all area news media-- newspapers, radio, television, and magazines. Last but not least, the editor should exchange with all members of his local chapter of the International Association of Business Communicators and with other editors, nationwide, who are in the same industry.

All extra coverage will be a tremendous help to the organization in getting across its story to the community, as well as to the company's specific public--usually the employees. The beauty of this extra coverage is that it can be done at a very low cost. The first and greatest cost is the makeready necessary to prepare the publication for printing. At very little cost, an additional hundred or so copies can be produced for the extra coverage. Once the mailing lists have been established, the added costs of sending another few hundred copies are small compared to the benefits to be gained.

RESEARCH FOR FEEDBACK AND STORIES

One of the big dangers the industrial editor must avoid is shooting in the dark. To avoid this, he must keep his finger on the pulse of the audience by actively seeking feedback.

Not only will the editor be able to test the impact of the publication through feedback and more formal research, but these methods quite likely will generate stories for future issues.

Probably the first bit of advice for the editor who wishes to be effective is to get out amongst the persons with whom he wants to communicate, whatever the audience.

If the publication is for employees, the editor must be visible to the employees on the production line. This means he should get out of the publication office and away from white-collar workers for significant periods.

The editor should learn the production workers by name, find out their hobbies, bowl with them, go on their golf outings, go fishing with them, and sit with them in the cafeteria at lunch or during coffee breaks. This way he will be visible and get meaningful feedback concerning the publication. He should avoid the ivory tower.

Formal research should be carried out, to get an accurate gauge of the impact the publication has on the audience.

For research of readership, the editor should go to a professional for advice, making sure the professional is one who has done opinion sampling in the field of publications. Research is most likely to be valid if it is done by an organization having no connection with the editor's company. This means it is better to hire an independent organization to do the study. The editor doesn't have to hire Gallup or Harris. Sometimes he can locate competent research personnel at a nearby university.

The value of the research is going to depend upon the direction in which the questioning is aimed. Many industrial editors are conned into using research to prove just how popular the publication is, which basically is almost beside the point. The crucial questions the editor wants answered are:

1. Is the publication read?

2. Is the reader absorbing the message?

3. Is the publication credible?

This means the survey must ask specific questions concerning content in recent publications. Also, questions must be posed to learn the reader reaction to this content. As noted before, it is almost irrelevant whether readers prefer bowling scores to stories on economic subjects, or articles on cooking to those on company expansions. This type of questioning tells the editor nothing.

If the questionnaire is going to poll reader preference, it should be along the lines of, for example: Q. Which of these sub-

jects would you like to learn more about through the publication--
new safety devices, company expansion plans, new products, etc?

After the research questionnaire has been administered and
the results tabulated, the editor should have the findings fully
explained to him or his supervisor. The mere accumulation of data
is meaningless unless a knowledgeable person can tabulate and in-
terpret the data. Also, there should be a pre-study decision of
what action to take after the findings have been interpreted.

Again, it is useless to take a survey unless it leads to something. There should be a follow-up on the basis of the findings
so that the editor can work to eliminate the weak spots of the publication and make it a more effective communications tool. There
should be one or more stories printed in the publication telling
readers of the findings.

Research for the generation of stories is less sophisticated
and can be carried out by the editor. There is, of course, the
everyday feedback in which persons may pop into the office and suggest stories. There is also the editor's routine calling on key
individuals in the organization to find out what is going on.

Aside from this, the editor will need more formal methods of
gaining story information. This can be done by surveys.

One of the prime groups for such a survey is the retirees.
There actually is no good way in which retirees can be contacted
except by mail. Therefore, from time to time, say every second or
third year, a survey should be mailed to the retirees; included

should be a request for some recent pictures. Then the information can be used for either a series of stories or a special edition.

For the employee group, salesmen, dealers, etc., the questionnaire probably should be much more extensive. The editor should design the form so he finds out the hobbies and community or civic involvement; he should mention specifically as many types of involvement as he can. These questionnaires should be administered by the supervisors of the various individuals; and every employee, dealer, salesman, etc., should be accounted for. This method means there is a chance to improve rapport between the supervisor and those for whom he is responsible.

The returns from such a survey should furnish the editor a gold mine of information concerning off-the-job activities of the persons involved. The results can be used in a special edition for employee recognition or for a continuing flow of stories over a period of several editions. (A sample questionnaire is shown at the end of the chapter.)

Research is a tool which every editor should have in his bag of tricks. If the editor lacks a basic knowledge of research methods, it would be well worth his time to take some research courses in a nearby university. The value of such courses would immediately become apparent to the individual. A communicator who communicates in only one direction and does not seek feedback cannot be effective.

COMMUNITY ACTIVITIES

Name_____Dept._____

Address_____City_____

Service Date_____Classification_____

    I participate in the following community activities. (Please give full name of organization and type of service given. Use back of sheet if necessary.)

CITY OFFICIAL: Mayor_____Councilman_____Fireman_____Policeman_____

Other_____. How long have you held this job?_____.

YOUTH ACTIVITY: Boy Scouts _____Girl Scouts_____Little League_____

   YMCA_____YWCA_____Other_____.

   What is your title?_____.

   How long have you held this job?_____.

CHURCH: Minister_____Lay preacher_____Sunday School teacher_____

   Elder_____Other_____.

   How long have you held this job?_____.

SERVICE GROUP: Izaak Walton_____Kiwanis_____Rotary_____Masons_____

   Optimists_____KC_____KP_____Nurse's Aid_____Hospital Volunteer_____

   Other_____.

   What is your title?_____.

   How long have you held this job?_____.

MILITARY: National Guard_____Reserve Unit_____Legion_____VFW_____

   Other_____.

   What is name of unit?_____.

   What is your title?_____.

   How long have you held this job?_____.

Fig. 38--Example of questionnaire. Example continues on next page.

COMMUNITY ACTIVITIES

SCHOOL: PTA_____Alumni Assn._____Fund Raising_____

   Other_____.

   What is your title?_____.

   How long have you held this job?_____.

CHARITY: United Campaign_____Red Cross_____Salvation Army_____.

   Legal Aid_____ Travelers Aid _____Other_____.

   What is your title?_____.

   How long have you held this job?_____.

PROFESSIONAL OR FRATERNAL: Eagles_____Elks_____Medical_____

   Nursing_____Other_____.

   What is your title?_____.

   How long have you held this job?_____.

Family:

Tell us something about your family

Fig. 38 (Continued)

Chapter

21

TAILORING THE MATERIAL TO THE AUDIENCE

A company publication is not necessarily edited for employees. Although employee publications are the most usual form of house journal, the company has other publics. If the organization wants to communicate in a meaningful manner, each public should have its own distinctive publication.

Examples of other publics are salesmen, stockholders, customers, dealers, salaried employees, and the general public.

An organization may not have the money to tailor a special publication for each audience. In this case, the company must decide which publics should be reached by publications, then tailor one for each audience. It is almost futile to try to do a good job of communicating by using one publication to reach all publics.

The reason is that the interests of each public vary at least slightly from those of any other.

The employee wants to know what the company is doing, why the company is doing it, and how this will affect his job.

The salesman cares little about fringe benefits affecting production employees or the need for safety equipment around machinery, etc. What the salesman needs and desires above all else is tips from the company which will help him sell the product.

The sales publication will use success stories featuring the top salesmen, with emphasis on:

* Ways in which they are able to overcome customer resistance.
* Ways in which they are better able to serve the customers.
* Which approaches have worked best for the top salesmen.
* Which aspects of the product the salesman should play up in the presentation.
* How the salesman makes the maximum use of his time with the customer.

There are, of course, stories about sales contests and the nice prizes which will go to the winners.

The stockholder cares little about the production problems at the factories or the constant battle of the salesmen to meet their quotas. The stockholder is mainly interested in moves by the company to make the entire operation more efficient. Of prime interest to the stockholder is the return on investment and the amount of quarterly dividend. The stockholder is secondarily interested in the long-term outlook for the company and whether it means there will be greater or smaller returns on his investment.

The dealer, although marginally interested in the problems of production and sales and somewhat more interested in the stock's earnings record and potential, is most interested in learning how to increase customer traffic into the store. So, instead of stories about fringe benefits, a dealer publication will have stories about building attractive displays, increasing customer traffic, and having gimmicks to hold the customer in the store so the clerks can give them a sales pitch. One dealer does this by handing the customer a cup of very hot coffee. The coffee can't be drunk immediately so, while it cools, the customer is given a sales talk.

The recognition stories in dealer publications would feature dealers who are very successful. The reasons for running such stories are:

1. To spur other dealers into doing better so they may be featured in the publication.

2. To point out to other dealers some of the innovations used by the successful dealer so the less successful ones may emulate him and, hopefully, become more successful themselves.

The major auto companies formerly had very successful customer magazines. The theory behind these publications was that the customer's car was going to last for several years of trouble-free operations. To keep the customer thinking of the manufacturer, the company would mail the customer a nice monthly magazine. Thus, the monthly publication served as a reminder that the company greatly valued the customer's business. Therefore, when the customer was ready to buy a new car--the theory went--he would be much more inclined to buy another car of the same make.

217

The major emphasis of these auto company customer magazines was well-written feature stories about tourist attractions in America and Canada. The companies reasoned that customers would be motivated to drive to these places for a visit. The motor company hoped to encourage greater use of the product and hasten the day when the customer would return to buy a new car. An example of such a journal is the Ford Times, which still appears monthly.

In some companies, the employee audience is so large and diverse that one overall publication simply cannot do the job of communicating with all employees.

This is especially true with organizations in which there are not only production workers with little education, but also technical or research employees with several college degrees. Some companies now edit one publication for production employees and another for salaried employees. Some will even have one publication for the management team, a second for the engineers and technical workers, and a third for the salaried employees who do not fit either category.

Another trend is for an organization to split its employee publication effort into geographical editions. Often, there is a corporate-wide publication for all employees. A local publication is edited for each large installation outside of the headquarters area.

Closely related to employee publications are association journals. An association is an organization which has few employees but many members. In this case, the publication is devoted to educating the members about organization goals. The editor seeks to hold members and gain new ones.

No matter what type of publication, the editor must make certain the audience is sharply defined and the material tailored to fit that specific audience.

The editor can best do this by making a thorough study of the audience and having sharply-defined goals, before attempting to communicate with it.

The surest way of doing an excellent job of serving the audience is to ascertain its needs and then fill them.

Chapter

22

THE FUTURE—THE EDITOR'S CHANGING JOB

The world moves, and we have to move with it. No one can stand still. A person either moves forward or falls behind.

So it is with the company editor. If he doesn't keep up with the trends of the times, he will find himself shunted onto a side-track, or his area eliminated or taken over by someone more up to date; or he may be fired.

It is not enough that an editor or staff is doing an excellent job with the publication. He needs to look constantly at what other organizations are doing, assess trends, then up-date procedures to stay ahead of obsolescence.

Many editors and/or publication programs already have charge of auxiliary information functions. It is well for the editor to keep constant watch to see what new devices or programs are available.

One method for the editor to keep current is to attend state, regional, or national conferences of the International Association of Business Communicators. These conferences usually have some part of the program aimed at trends.

Another way to prepare for the future is to continue one's education, if only through short courses, in the latest communications techniques and devices. If possible, the editor should keep aware of advances in printing, electronic communications, and such innovations as the four-day week, three-day week, and twelve-hour day.

The shorter work weeks make it harder for the editor and the organization to communicate with employees. How do you reach employees when they aren't at work and they aren't at home?

Here are some innovations in employee communications which have been added to the corporate information arsenal:

* Video taped information shows. The tapes are mailed to all installations for viewing by employees. In some cases, the employees view the tapes through a TV monitor on company time.

* Page advertisements in local newspapers. It is hoped these reach not only the employees who live in the community but the general public as well. One drawback is that advertising is less believable than a news story.

* Information shows over local television stations. Companies sometimes think these are a more effective way to reach the employee audience as well as the general public.

* The company message aired by radio.

* Slide shows put together for viewing by visitors.

* Company films, 35-mm or 8-mm. These are to be loaned to

groups and shown to employees. These films usually deal
with some phase of the company's operations.

* Telephone information centers which employees can call to
get answers to questions concerning the company's operations.

Among the more unusual devices are the Goodyear blimps and the
Firestone sponsorship of bowling, golf and auto racing.

No one can really forecast what the future will bring, but the
wise person can early spot an effective information innovation and
learn to use it.

The knowledgeable editor should keep watch on such developments
as cable television, outdoor advertising, taped messages, data
processing machines, etc.

The editor should be cautioned that most of the other information media are probably less effective than the publication(s) in
communicating with the organization's publics.

However, the editor should not overlook or ignore other possible communication devices, but use them as supplements to the
house journal--the backbone of the information program.

The house journal has many things in its favor in competition
for attention. In the first place, it is written down and not
ephemeral as are television or radio messages.

The house journal can cover a subject in much more depth than
a three-minute radio or television spot. Then, too, the employee
knows where to contact the editor for rebuttal in case he wishes to

take issue with an item in the house journal. But how does one take issue with a television spot or a slide presentation? Also, there always is the chance the employee is going to have his picture in the publication. The chances are slim of the employee's picture, or that of a friend, appearing in a slide presentation or TV show.

Besides which, to the employee, salesman, etc., the house journal is an old friend which keeps putting in an appearance regularly. It is just as though someone from the company has dropped in for a visit to let the reader know he is appreciated. That is why the company publication usually has such loyalty and credibility in the minds of the readers.

So . . . the company should hang on to its publication as a powerful medium in the arsenal of communications. However, the editor should be knowledgeable of the strengths and weaknesses of these other supplements in the same arsenal. Those other methods of communications should be used whenever it is appropriate and to the company's advantage.

Chapter

23

SOME LEGAL ASPECTS

Although the industrial editor is not so likely to commit libel (written defamation) as the newspaper reporter, it is still a good idea to be aware of legal restrictions which apply to the company publication.

The editor need not become a lawyer with knowledge of all the legal nuances involving publication. However, he should be aware of the simple defenses against libel.

The laws of libel differ from state to state. No one should consider himself an expert on libel unless he holds a law degree and has practiced in the state for a number of years. However, the following defenses offer a good rule of thumb:

1. Truth.--If the facts of the story are 100 percent correct, there is little chance of the editor's losing a libel suit; however, a story must not have been used maliciously. For instance, an individual's unsavory past should not be brought to light in a publication after the person has lived an exemplary life for many years.

2. Fair Comment.--The material is not libelous if it is a

fair comment upon an individual's public performance.
For instance, the editor might comment with impunity about
the legislative record of a congressman or upon any public official as long as he confines himself to the public
performance. Under no circumstances should the editor comment on the individual's personal life. (A possible exception might be a laudatory feature story written with
the subject's consent.)

3. Privilege.--Privilege means there are certain public documents and proceedings which can be quoted even though the
material is libelous or constitutes written defamation.
Such privileged material would include speeches made in
Congress, state legislatures, or testimony given in court.

The best course to take, if there is the slightest doubt, is
to consult legal counsel. Almost every organization has a lawyer
employed full time or on a retainer basis. This individual is being paid to give legal advice, so the editor should have a working
agreement that the lawyer will examine stories to make sure such
will not involve the publication in a law suit.

Because of the nature of employee publications, most are virtually free of the possibility of being involved in a libel suit.
However, there are two areas--labor-management relations and trade-
marks--which can give the company publication trouble.

In the realm of libel, good judgment and care usually keep
the daily- and weekly-newspaper reporter reasonably free of diffi-

culty. By the same token, reasonable exercise of the same good judgment and care should guarantee the company editor against being involved in libel suits.

It is through error that the greatest danger lies. Ambiguities, typographical errors, and even careless handling of some personal items may result in litigation or at least embarrassment to everyone concerned. Sound editorial procedures, carefully administered, represent the best safeguard against such unfortunate occurrences.

The greatest danger of lawbreaking by the company editor comes in the field of labor-management relations. It is not the province of this book to devote a lot of space to the nuances of the various federal laws concerning labor-management relations. One problem is that federal laws and court decisions in this field can change dramatically in a short time.

It is sufficient to warn the editor to obtain a copy of the Wagner Act of 1935 and the Taft-Hartley Act of 1947 and keep such on file for ready reference. Whenever the editor has any story which deals with labor-management relations, it would be a very good idea to present the material to the company lawyer for close scrutiny. It is also a good idea for the editor to talk with the legal counsel, from time to time, for a briefing on changes in labor laws and court decisions.

The same advice applies to the Landrum-Griffin Act of 1959.

The company publication should lead the way in the protection of trademarks. Whenever the marks are used in copy, they should be given distinctive typographical dress to make them stand out. Certainly the trademarks should always be set with the initial letters capitalized, if that is the way the trademark is registered. The company's trademarks should never be used lower case in its publication, unless that is the way they are registered.

Some publications use an asterisk and an appropriate footnote to draw the readers' attention to the registration of the mark. Others list all of the company's trademarks in the masthead or flag.

The editor who starts a house journal or company publication should have the legal counsel make a search of trademarks to see if the proposed name is registered with the federal government. If the name is not already registered, it might be advisable to register it. This would eliminate the possibility that some other company might later use the same name and register it as a trademark. In this case, the editor who first used the name could be legally enjoined from further use of it.

The editor should, by all means, copyright his publication if use is made of free-lance material. This is especially important if the free lance is a well-known literary, artistic, or photographic "name."

The protection of the trademarks is a must for everyone connected with the organization. Unless the organization protects the trademarks, they can become generic terms, meaning that any organization which desires can use them.

Trademarks may be registered with the U.S. Patent Office, Washington, D.C. Registration is for 20 years and renewable for 20-year periods. For registration to continue after application, the mark must be used in commerce regulated by the federal government. An affidavit of such use must be submitted during the fifth year following the application.

Industrial editors do not agree concerning the use of copyrights for their publications. Most editors feel it is good to have their material reach the widest possible audience. For this reason, these editors usually do not seek copyright and will freely give permission to anyone who desires to use the material.

On the other hand, some editors want their literary efforts protected by copyright, to assure that an editor will be duly compensated by anyone who wants to use his material.

This means the editor who desires to use material from another publication should examine the publication to see if it is copyrighted. One should never use copyrighted material without first seeking the permission of the publisher. There may be a fee charged for such use.

Even though material is not copyrighted, common courtesy dictates seeking permission of the publisher before using material borrowed from another publication.

Of course, even though material is copyrighted, those elements which are common knowledge or in general everyday usage can be used without permission.

Under the so-called common law of the United States, literary property in an unpublished work is automatically protected from the instant it is created.

The common-law protection exists until the author (1) dedicates his work to the public or (2) obtains a statutory copyright.

Any authorized general publication constitutes dedication of the work to public use. Common-law rights are thereby lost. Unless the author obtains a copyright under the federal statute, the work goes into the public domain at the time of publication.

To obtain a post-publication copyright under Title 17 of the U.S. Code, the following steps must be completed:

1. Copies must be produced with a copyright notice.

2. The work must be published.

3. The claim must be registered with the Copyright Office.

The requirement of the first step is met when the notice of copyright is put on the title page or the first page of the text. That notice must include the following: "Copyright," Copr.," or the letter "C" enclosed in a circle; the year of publication; and the name of the copyright owner.

According to the copyright act, the second step is completed as of the date "when copies of the first authorized edition are placed on sale, sold, or publicly distributed by the proprietor of the copyright. . . ."

Registration requires the completion of an application form which is available from the Copyright Office. This form is sent to the Copyright Office along with two copies of the work and a $4 fee. Any fee should be in the form of a money order, check, or bank draft, payable to the "Register of Copyrights," the Library of Congress, Washington, D.C.

It should be understood that it is the act of publication with notice of copyright that produces the protection; the Copyright Office merely registers claims; it does not grant copyrights. Therefore, the protection starts immediately with publication.

Protection can last for 56 years--28 with the original application, and an additional 28 if the application for renewal is filed during the twenty-eighth year.

The three-step process for obtaining copyright protection must be repeated for every issue of the publication. It is not possible to obtain one copyright that will provide protection for all future issues or works of an author.

A notice of copyright should not be included in a publication unless the registration with the Copyright Office is going to be completed. Unless the protection afforded by the Copyright Act is sincerely desired, a statutory copyright should not be obtained. If, however, it is obtained, the owner should guard against unauthorized use of the copyrighted material.

Infringement of copyright consists of substantial copying of the protected material. But if the author quotes a small amount of the copyrighted material for the purpose of commenting about the work, this may be done without the author's permission.

However, as mentioned before, ethically and legally, it is a good idea to seek the permission of the author before borrowing written material, whether or not the material is copyrighted.

Copyright protection is good only in the United States and those nations with which we have reciprocity.

GLOSSARY

Some of the terms contained in this glossary are common to all printing; others are distinctive to industrial journalism alone. Of those listed, some have nothing to do with printing, per se, but apply to business. Although all of the words are listed in standard English (American) dictionaries, the author has tried to define the words in their industrial context. There has been no attempt to seek out and define every word used in the text; after all, this is not a dictionary of terms. Anyone who is competent to edit a company publication should be familiar with most of the words used. It is assumed that the user of this text will, as a matter of course, have in his possession and use frequently an up-to-date dictionary.

Action Line Column. Similar to newspaper action line column. Usually consists of gripes or complaints against the company or suggestions concerning working conditions.

Art (artwork). Any illustration--picture, line drawing. Almost any element in a publication other than copy.

Association Journal. A publication (house journal) edited by the association for mailing to members.

Audience. A specific group to which you address (aim) a communication; a public.

Bacon's Publicity Checker. A reference listing of mass media.

Balance. The editor's achievement of all objectives in an issue.

Banner. A headline which extends the entire width of a page.

Bindery. A place where printed materials are bound.

Body Type. The basic type used as text for most of the stories in a magazine or newspaper.

Bound. Enclosed in a binding or cover, such as a book or magazine.

Box. A short newspaper or magazine item usually set off with rules on four sides.

Business Paper. A journal, edited by an independent publishing company, which carries news and features about an industry or a segment of an industry; a trade journal.

Business Press. An association of trade journal editors and publishers; The American Business Press.

Camera Ready. In offset printing, material which is ready for the cameraman to reproduce on light-sensitive sheets; in final form.

Caption. One line of editorial explanation above or below a picture.

Chain of Command. The normal progression of authority in an organization from bottom to top.

Checking Copy. A printed piece of copy used to make corrections.

Clearances. The pre-publication checking of material by several company officials to insure the material's accuracy and safeguard company secrets.

Column. Section of newspaper page. Most newspaper columns are about 2 inches wide.

Column Inch. An inch of copy one column wide.

Communicator. One who sends or receives messages; editor, writer, etc.

Company Publication. A house journal; a company-produced newspaper or magazine tailored to reach a public of the company.

Composition. Text which has been set into type.

Consumer Publication. A general circulation newspaper or magazine.

Copy. The text of a story or advertisement; the part of a publication which consists of text.

Copyright. The exclusive right to publish a literary work.

Copyright Act. The government legislation providing for copyrights.

Copyright Office. The government office which registers copyrights.

Corporate Hierarchy. The corporation table of organization.

Created Event. An artificially designed occurrence such as an open house, production milestone, or service anniversary dreamed up by a practitioner. (The other kind of occurrence is a spontaneous event, such as an accident, fire, explosion, etc.)

Cut. Art in a form ready for printing; engraving.

Cutlines. The editorial explanation under a picture. Usually consists of two or more lines of type.

Document. Any paper or book conveying information; to equip with references.

Dummy. A pattern volume of a printing job in which all of the text and art are positioned as a guide to the printer or paste-up artist.

Edition. All the copies of one printing of a publication.

Editorial. A publication article which gives the editor's views.

Employee Publication. A house journal or company publication edited for employees.

Engraving. An image etched into metal, usually a picture used for printing.

External Publication. A company publication edited for a non-company public, such as customers.

Feature. A non-timely newspaper or magazine story of little intrinsic news value, but considerable emotional appeal.

Feedback. Audience reaction conveyed to the communicator via letters, phone calls, or conversations.

Filler. A short item used in a publication to fill space.

Flag. The name of a newspaper on its front page.

Focus. Where interest is concentrated; to adjust a lens so the visual image is clear.

Format. The shape, size, and general makeup of a publication.

Gauge. A graduated scale for measuring.

Generic. Characteristic of a whole group; not protected by trademark.

Gimmick. A new and ingenious scheme or angle.

Glossies. Photographs.

Graphic Arts. Any of the skills involved in the printing process.

Head (Headline) Schedule. The kinds and families of type used by
     publication or available at a job shop.

Headline Type. The type used in a headline, several sizes larger
     than body type; display type.

House Journal. A Company or organizational publication.

I.A.B.C. International Association of Business Communicators.

Illustrations. Pictures or drawings.

Industrial Editor. The editor of a company publication; the house
     journal editor.

In-House Printer. A printing shop operated by the company which
     employs the industrial editor.

Internal Publication. A company publication or house journal which
     goes to an internal public, such as employees.

Interpretive Article. An article which is basically explanatory
     rather than expository.

Issue. All the copies of a publication in a single printing.

Job Shop. A printing shop which specializes in contract printing.

Journal. A newspaper or magazine.

Layout. Dummy; the final arrangement of matter to be printed.

Lead. The first few sentences or paragraphs of a news story.

Letterpress. Direct printing from raised surfaces.

Line Gauge. A pica stick; a gauge for measuring printing, cali-
     brated in picas.

Line Measure. The width of a line of type in picas.

Line Screen. The relative coarseness or fineness of a screen used
     in making photographic engravings.

Makeup. The arrangement of items on the various pages of a dummy.

Masthead. Boxed material in a publication, listing title, owner-
ship, and other pertinent data concerning the publication.

Media. The plural of medium.

Medium. A means of effecting or conveying something.

Monitor. Regulate or control.

Nameplate. Flag; the newspaper's name on page one.

Negatives. The filmed image from which pictures are contact printed
or enlarged as glossies.

News Bureau. An information service which prepares and sends out
stories concerning the organization.

Offset. A method of indirect printing from "cold type."

Opinion Leader. A person who influences the thinking of others.

Outdoor Advertising. Billboards.

Out of Register. In color printing, the inaccurate meeting or
overlapping of two or more colors.

Overset. Material set into type but not used in the publication.

Pi. Scrambled type.

Pica. A measure of type; one-sixth of an inch, or 12 points.

Pica Measure. The width of a line of type expressed in picas.

Pica Stick. The line gauge used to measure type. Calibrated in
picas.

Point. 1/72 inch; a measure of type.

Poll. Seek public opinion by formal research.

Practitioner. A person engaged in an occupation, profession, or
other line of expertise.

Press Run. All of the copies produced at one printing.

Privilege. Defense against libel. Libelous material can be printed
when it has been stated in certain public meetings or when it
is contained in certain public documents.

Proprietor. An owner and/or operator.

Public. A cohesive group with a common objective, which the organization tries to influence; for example, employees, stockholders,
etc.

Public Domain. Can be used by anyone at no charge; not protected
by copyright.

Public Relations. The various aspects of influencing the opinions
of publics through the use of two-way communications.

Purchased Service. A service which the company has to buy outside
the company.

Purchasing Agent. The individual in a company who has charge of
all buying.

Purge Mailing List. Bring a mailing list up to date by correcting
addresses, removing names of deceased, etc.

Questionnaire. A form on which is printed a list of questions;
used in polling or formal research.

Radio Spot. A short announcement over radio--often 10 seconds.

Readership Study. A formal study to discover how well the publication is read.

Register. In color printing, the alignment of colors printed over
each other.

Routing. The removal by sawing of the unwanted part of an engraving.

Scale. Figure out the proportions of a picture to be engraved.

Screen. A device used in engraving. The coarser the paper, the coarser the screen, and vice versa.

Specifications (Specs). A detailed listing of particulars to be followed by suppliers in performing a service.

Spot News. News obtained at the scene of the event, hence fresh, live news. Unexpected event.

Standard Rate and Data Service. Reference books listing advertising, circulation, and other rates and data of various media, such as newspapers, magazines, etc.

Statutory Copyright. A copyright which has been registered by the Register of Copyrights.

Tabloid. A half-size newspaper.

Tear Sheet. A sheet torn from a publication and sent to an advertiser to show how the ad appeared in print.

Title Page. Page which bears the book's title.

Top of the Head, Back of the Head. Writing or speaking extemporaneously.

Trade Journal. A publication which serves the interests of a specific industry or trade.

Trademark. A mark, symbolizing the maker of the product, registered with the U.S. Government.

Type Face. A specific size and kind of type, such as 14-point Bodoni bold.

Type Family. A family or variety of type, such as Bodoni, Baskerville, Caslon, etc.

Type Size. The vertical size of the base of the type, such as 8

   point, 9 point, etc. For example, 24-point type means that

   the base measures 24/72 or 1/3 of an inch from top to bottom.

Web Perfecting Press. A rotary press which prints simultaneously

   on both sides of the paper or web.

BIBLIOGRAPHY

The Complete Editor from A to Z
   Walter G. Anderson
   Published by the author

      Contains examples of different ways to handle a variety of
      topics normally taken care of by an industrial editor.

Editing the Small Magazine
   Rowena Ferguson
   Columbia Paperback

      Outlines the steps taken by the editor and staff in producing
      a small magazine, from idea to finished publication.

Effective Public Relations, 4th ed.
   Cutlip and Center
   Prentice-Hall, Inc.

      Offers a wide-ranging overview of the entire spectrum of ex-
      pertise in the field of public relations. This is the stand-
      ard college text for public relations.

The Graphics of Communication, 2nd ed.
   Turnbull and Baird
   Holt, Rinehart & Winston, Inc.

      A standard textbook in the use of graphics, layout, and de-
      sign.

Ink on Paper

Edmund Arnold
Harper & Row, Publishers

A definitive text on the effective use of type and art in laying out newspaper pages.

Modern Magazine Editing

Robert Root
William C. Brown Company, Publishers

A valuable book on magazine editing and production. This was, for a long time, the standard text in college magazine courses.

Publication Design

Roy Paul Nelson
William C. Brown Company, Publishers

A book on layout, design, and graphics for newspapers and magazines.

Public Relations Handbook

Philip Lesly, ed.
Prentice-Hall, Inc.

A massive collection of public relations expertise written by professionals for professionals. Each chapter is by someone who has specialized in his specific area of public relations practice.

The Ragan Report

Lawrence Ragan and Associates
Published by the author

A periodical providing tips for the industrial editor.

INDEX

Copy
    clearing, 180
    following, 186
    logging, 185, 201
    marking, 181

Copyreading, 183
    symbols, 200

Copyright, 228, 229, 230, 231

Corporate image, 119

Created event, 139

Cropping
    L's, 199
    pictures, 198

Customer letters, 101

D

Deadlines, setting, 174

Dealer publication, 216

Dealer recognition, 127

Depression, 26

Distribution, 193

Down-style flag, 102

Dummy, preparing, 188

E

Eagleton, Thomas, 27

Economic education, 109

Editorial board, 86

Effective PR, 80

Empire State Building, 42

Employee magazines, study of, 2

Employee recognition, 114, 115, 124

Employee survey, 142

Energy conservation, 116

Establishing need, 8

F

Factory News, 2

Factory start-up, 5

Feature material sources, 145

Features, 152

Field sales publication, 99

File everything, 178

Fillers, 151

Flesch, Rudolph, 42

Frame of reference, 27

G

Galley proofs, 187

Gebbie House Magazine Directory, 1

General-ly Speaking, 107

Goals, 26, 31

Grievance story, 105

Gunning, Robert, 42

19